AF417896

The Removal of Blame from The Great Imams

Taqiuddin Ibn Taymiyyah

Dar Ul Thaqafah

DAR UL THAQAFAH

https://twitter.com/darulthaqafah
www.darulthaqafah.com

Also available from

MaktabaIslamia Publications
www.maktabaislamia.com
info@maktabaislamia.com
www.twitter.com/maktabaislamia

2022 CE – 1443 H

Translation of the Qur'ān

It should be perfectly clear that the Qur'ān is only authentic in its original language, Arabic. Since perfect translation of the Qur'ān is impossible, we have used the translation of the meaning of the Qur'ān throughout the book, as the result is only a crude meaning of the Arabic text.

Qur'ānic verses appear in speech marks proceeded by a reference to the Surah and verse number. Sayings (*Hadith*) of Prophet Muhammad (saw) appear in inverted commas along with reference to the Hadith Book and its Reporter.

The Removal of Blame from the Great *Imāms*: An Annotated Translation of Ibn Taymiyyah's. *Rafʿ al-Malām ʿan al-Aʾimmat al-Aʿlām*

AḤMAD IBN ʿABD AL-ḤALĪM IBN TAYMIYYAH

Tr. and Ann. ABDUL HAKIM AL-MATROUDI

I

INTRODUCTION

Aḥmad b. ʿAbd al-Ḥalīm b. ʿAbd al-Salām b. ʿAbd Allāh b. Abī ʾl-Qāsim al-Khiḍr b. Muḥammad b. Taymiyyah[1] (661–728/1263–1328) is arguably the most distinguished and influential medieval Ḥanbalī jurist[2] and perhaps one of the most prolific among them.[3] He was born in Ḥarrān (present day Turkey) and lived during the era of the first Mamlūks (648–784/1250–1382). However, he was forced to move from his native region and take up residence in Damascus due to the Mongol onslaught from the East.[4] He lived in turbulent

---

[1] For a discussion of the possible reasons for him being given the name 'Taymiyyah,' see, Abdul Hakim Ibrahim al-Matroudi, *The Hanbali School of Law and Ibn Taymiyyah: Conflict or Conciliation* (London: Routledge Curzon, 2006), 199–200 f.

[2] ʿAbd al-Raḥmān b. Aḥmad Ibn Rajab, *al-Dhayl ʿalā Ṭabaqāt al-Ḥanābilah* (Beirut: Dār al-Maʿrifah, n.d.), 2: 388–91; ʿUmar b. ʿAlī al-Bazzār, *al-Aʿlām al-ʿAliyyah fī Manāqib Ibn Taymiyyah* (Beriut: al-Maktab al-Islāmī, 1400 AH), 18–20, 40, 77.

[3] The total number of works written by Ibn Taymiyyah are not known exactly but there is agreement that he was a prolific author. See, ʿAbd al-Ḥayy b. Aḥmad Ibn al-ʿImād, *Shadharāt al-Dhahab fī Akhbār Man Dhahab* (Damsacus-Beirut: Dār Ibn Kathīr, 1992), 8: 147. See also, Muḥammad b. Aḥmad al-Dhahabī, *Dhayl Taʾrīkh al-Islām* (Riyadh: Dār al-Mughnī, 1990) 326; Muḥammad b. Aḥmad Ibn ʿAbd al-Hādī, *al-ʿUqūd al-Durriyyah min Manāqib Shaykh al-Islām Ibn Taymiyyah* (Riyadh: Maktabat al-Muaʾyyad, n.d.), 64–66; al-Bazzār, *al-Aʿlām*, 25–28; Muḥammad b. ʿAbd Allāh Ibn Rushayyiq, *Asmāʾ Muʾallafāt Shaykh al-Islām Ibn Taymiyyah* (Beirut: Dār al-Kitāb al-Jadīd, 1983), 8, (it is attributed mistakenly to Muḥammad b. Abī Bakr Ibn al-Qayyim, d. 751/1350); Marʿī b. Yūsuf al-Karmī, *al-Kawākib al-Duriyyah fī Manāqib al-Mujtahid Ibn Taymiyyah* (Beirut: Dār al-Gharb al-Islāmī, 1986), 78; and cf. al-Matroudi, *The Hanbali School of Law*, 23–30.

[4] Ibrāhīm b. Muḥammad Ibn Mufliḥ, *al-Maqsad al-Arshad fī Dhikr Aṣḥāb al-Imām Aḥmad* (Riyadh: Maktabat al-Rushd, 1410 AH), 1: 133.

1

times when Muslim political fragmentation was clearly visible. Moreover, legal fanaticism and doctrinal laxity prevailed in Muslim lands and he is historically portrayed as someone who sought to rectify both religious and political disparities and deviancies which led to open encounters with his contemporaries as well as to long spells in prison.[5]

Ibn Taymiyyah is often seen through a simplistic anti-rationalist prism, that is, as someone with strict and literal inclinations towards *Hadith* which he over emphasised and preferred to acceptance of broader legal theories and principles. The present text would suffice to undermine that view. *Raf' al-Malām 'an al-A'immat al-A'lām* is a short text in which the reader observes Ibn Taymiyyah as a jurist *par excellence*. In this treatise, which has a balanced tone and is couched in erudite language, he proceeds to argue as to why a *mujtahid* might depart from directly acting upon a *ḥadīth* text and follow instead his methodological principles (*uṣūl*). This forms the basis of his delineating the reasons underlying the disagreements found among Muslim jurists in general and their holding differing legal opinions and proffering divergent arguments in support of those opinions.

It is interesting that Ibn Taymiyyah turned down the request of some of his students to compose a treatise in the Science of Jurisprudence (*uṣūl al-fiqh*) which would contain all of his jurisprudential opinions and preferences in order to be used as a basis for issuing legal verdicts (*fatāwā*). He justified his refusal by pointing out that rulings on jurisprudential issues are based upon independent reasoning (*ijtihād*) and there is no harm for the subject of the law (*mukallaf*) to imitate a *mujtahid* for that purpose.[6] Thus, Ibn Taymiyyah did not see the existence of various jurisprudential approaches to be problematic; rather, he believed that the real problem lay in intolerance and fanaticism. In *Raf' al-Malām*, Ibn Taymiyyah pleads for tolerance by identifying the different possible causes for jurisprudential disagreements (*ikhtilāf*) and seeks to absolve the *mujtahid* of any blame in committing an error and/or in departing from a *ḥadīth* in his judgment.

No doubt, Ibn Taymiyyah's espousal of this position was an outcome of various contributory factors. In what follows, I hope to give to the reader a glimpse of Ibn Taymiyyah's life and thought which would hopefully provide some insight into the reasons underpinning this sensitivity. The first section of this Introduction will focus on some of the statements of his contemporaries as mentioned in the biographical sources, which reflect their opinions regarding Ibn Taymiyyah's "natural and acquired attributes." The next section will present some of the unique features of Ibn Taymiyyah's scholarship, such

---

[5] See, al-Matroudi, *The Hanbali School of Law*, 13–16.

[6] Al-Bazzār, *al-A'lām*, 35–37.

as his distinguished knowledge of *Ḥadīth* and jurisprudence and some of his opinions with regard to legal imitation (*taqlīd*) and *ijtihād*. The last section will draw attention to some of the salient points in *Rafʿ al-Malām* in the hope of presenting to the reader the sense and context of this treatise before finally offering a full translation of the original Arabic text.

The biographical sources extol the virtues of Ibn Taymiyyah and biographical works are replete with praise by his contemporaries, especially his students,[7] and also his successors.[8] He was fortunate that his father Shihāb al-Dīn ʿAbd al-Ḥalīm b. ʿAbd al-Salām (d. 682/1283) and his grandfather Majd al-Dīn ʿAbd al-Salām b. ʿAbd Allāh (d. 652/1254)—both distinguished legal scholars in their times—greatly contributed to his early learning. So thorough and intense was his early training that by the age of twenty or even earlier, he was issuing legal opinions within the Ḥanbalī School and according to the statement of the great Ḥanbalī jurist, Muḥammad b. Aḥmad Ibn ʿAbd al-Hādī (d. 744/1345), who was also Ibn Taymiyyah's student, the people of Damascus, where Ibn Taymiyyah lived, were dazzled by the intensity of his intelligence and acumen.[9] It is no wonder that while he was still a child, he was described as a "precocious genius."[10]

Ibn Taymiyyah had a phenomenal and prodigious memory and there would be very little he would read and fail to commit to memory.[11] Often he would memorize a large number of works in various branches of learning,[12] and ʿUmar b. ʿAlī al-Bazzār (d. 749/1348) remarked that it was rare to find a book which Ibn Taymiyyah did not know about.[13] His sharp and systematic memory enabled him to acquire knowledge of encyclopaedic proportions and Muḥammad b. ʿAlī al-Zamalkānī (727/1327) notes that when Ibn Taymiyyah would answer a question in one of the traditional disciplines, the listener would think that he did not know any other discipline due to the depth and comprehensive nature of his answer.[14] Even a cursory reading of Ibn

---

[7] His students include the most pre-eminent figures such as Ibn Kathīr, al-Dhahabī, Ibn Qayyim al-Jawziyyah, al-Bazzār and Ibn ʿAbd al-Hādī.

[8] Indeed, the sources also document the more controversial episodes of Ibn Taymiyyah's life especially his doctrinal conflicts and legal interpretations that have been discussed and treated elsewhere. See, Al-Matroudi, *The Hanbali School of Law*, 20–23 for an account of his admirers and detractors.

[9] Ibn ʿAbd al-Hādī, *al-ʿUqūd*, 3.

[10] Al-Bazzār, *al-Aʿlām*, 18–19 and al-Karmī, *al-Kawākib*, 53.

[11] See, Ibn al-ʿImād, *Shadharāta al-Dhahab*, 8: 144.

[12] See, Ibn ʿAbd al-Hādī, *al-ʿUqūd*, 6 and al-Bazzār, *al-Aʿlām*, 19.

[13] Ibid.

[14] Ibid., 7. For further details of the testimony of leading scholars regarding the breadth of his knowledge, see, Ibn ʿAbd al-Hādī, *al-ʿUqūd*, 3–26; al-Bazzār, *al-Aʿlām*, 22–31 and al-Karmī, *al-*

Taymiyyah's works reveals a thoroughness and an encompassing attention to detail, possible only on the basis of extensive knowledge and sharp understanding of the various Islamic and non-traditional disciplines.[15] As a leading scholar replied when asked about him, "I saw a man as though all the sciences [were laid] open before his eyes and he took as he wished."[16]

Ibn Taymiyyah not only read theology, Arabic grammar and semantics as well as exegesis (*tafsīr*), but he also became proficient in Algebra, logic, history and philosophy. As a result, he wrote polemical treatises refuting Aristotelian philosophy that had seeped into the academic life of his day.[17] Although it must be mentioned that thanks to his studies in logic, there are undeniable traces of its influence especially in his systematic presentation of arguments and his use of explicit reasoning from established premises.

Aside from the tributes paid to Ibn Taymiyyah's intellectual and scholarly qualities, the biographical sources also mention the strength and resolve of his character. Al-Bazzār, for example, describes Ibn Taymiyyah as "one of the most courageous people who he had not seen the likes of."[18] This courage is reflected in his long periods of detention in both Cairo and Damascus. Although Ibn Taymiyyah's detentions were extremely distressing for him, it is obvious that he was able to turn them to his advantage by concentrating on scholarly pursuits of teaching and writing.[19] This is perhaps

---

Kawākib, 55–72, 80–82.

[15] See, Al-Karmī, *al-Kawākib*, 71, 79; al-Bazzār, *al-Aʿlām*, 32; Ibn Rajab, *Dhayl*, 2: 389–393 and ʿAbd al-Raḥmān b. Ṣāliḥ al-Maḥmūd, *Mawqif Ibn Taymiyyah min al-Ashāʿirah* (Riyadh: Maktabat al-Rushd, 1995), 1: 262, 294.

[16] Muḥammad ʿAzīz Shams, et al, *al-Jāmiʿ fī Sīrat Shaykh al-Islām Ibn Taymiyyah Khilāl Sabʿat Qurūn* (Makkah: Dār ʿĀlam al-Fawāʾid, 1420 AH), 258. See also, Ibn al-ʿImād, *Shadharāt al-Dhahab*, 8: 146.

[17] See, Muḥammad b. ʿAlī al-Dāwūdī, *Ṭabaqāt al-Mufassirīn* (Beirut: Dār al-Kutub al-ʿIlmiyyah, 1983), 1: 49. Ibn Taymiyyah composed several works to refute Greek logic, most notable being his, *Naqd al-Manṭiq* (Cairo: Maktabat al-Sunnah al-Muḥammadiyyah, n.d.) and volume 9 of his, *Majmūʿ Fatāwā Shaykh al-Islam Aḥmad Ibn Taymiyyah* (Riyadh: Dār ʿĀlam al-Kutub, 1991), [henceforth referred to as "*Fatāwā*"]. It is not difficult to see the reason underpinning his scathing attack as it was through inheriting Greek logic that Islamic philosophers espoused the doctrine of the eternity of the world; an incongruent account of the nature and attributes of God; the Platonic cosmological hierarchy with mediatory roles of the 'Intelligences'; a deficient notion of prophethood; the creation of the Qurʾān, etc. All these teachings, as espoused by the philosophers, stood in stark contrast to what Ibn Taymiyyah perceived to be the *Sunnī* or orthodox position that was dictated by the text of the Qurʾān and the *Sunnah*. See, Wael B. Hallaq, *Ibn Taymiyyah against the Greek Logicians* (Oxford: Clarendon Press, 1993), xii.

[18] Al-Bazzār, *al-Aʿlām*, 69 and al-Karmī, *al-Kawākib*, 91.

[19] This can be seen clearly through the vast number of extant treatises. Ibn ʿAbd al-Hādī, *al-ʿUqūd*, 51; Ibn Rajab, *al-Dhayl*, 2: 403, he observes that the majority of Ibn Taymiyyah's books were written in prison often without any references to consult and use. See also, al-Bazzār, *al-*

what Ibn Taymiyyah meant when he declared, "There is great benefit in it," when he was informed of his imprisonment.[20] Indeed, apart from the opportunity provided by these detentions to concentrate on scholarly pursuits, there is no doubt that these detentions also added to his fame.[21]

Important for the comprehension of the present text is the fact that Ibn Taymiyyah was especially noted for his knowledge in *Hadīth* and *fiqh*. With regard to *Hadīth*, Ibn Taymiyyah was not a jurist who had just a smattering of it. Far from that, he had studied it under several eminent *Hadīth* specialists (*muhaddithūn*) of his time. So extensive was his knowledge of *Hadīth* that it evoked the admiration of the most distinguished *Hadīth* scholars. Muhammad b. Ahmad al-Dhahabī (d. 748/1348), for example, remarked that if someone claimed that if any particular *hadīth* was not known to Ibn Taymiyyah, it could not be counted as a *hadīth*, his claim will be true.[22] In addition, Yūsuf b. 'Abd al-Rahmān al-Mizzī (d. 742/1341) asserts that he had not seen anyone more knowledgeable than Ibn Taymiyyah in Qur'ān and *Sunnah*.[23]

Ibn Taymiyyah's vast knowledge of *Hadīth* had a significant impact on his opinions.[24] It enabled him to declare in plain terms that a correct text does not conflict with correct reason,[25] and that several opinions in some of the schools of law had "no supporting proofs,"[26] or at best, they were supported

---

A'lām, 24; Muhammad b. 'Alī al-Shawkānī, *al-Badr al-Tāli' bi Mahāsin man ba'd al-Qarn al-Sābi'* (Cairo: Matba'at al-Sa'ādah, 1348), 1: 72, he states that if Ibn Taymiyyah had not been confronted by all the excessive trials (*mihan*) he would have presented more research. It could be also safely concluded that if Ibn Taymiyyah had not faced all these *mihan*, he would have probably directed more of his attention to other areas such as jurisprudence and its fundamentals or *Hadīth*.

[20] Al-Karmī, *al-Kawākib*, 149.

[21] Al-Bazzār, *al-A'lām*, 78.

[22] See, Ibn al-'Imād, *Shadharāt al-Dhahab*, 8: 145.

[23] See, Ibn 'Abd al-Hādī, *al-'Uqūd*, 7.

[24] For instance, he used to hold the opinion that when the water is less than *qullatayn*, it becomes impure as soon as it meets dirt even if its smell, colour or taste has not been changed. However, later on he changed his opinion concerning this issue as we find him denying the use of *qullatayn* as a measure. This change in Ibn Taymiyyah's opinion seems to reflect the change in his knowledge of *hadīth*, as he later arrived at the conclusion that the *hadīth* of *qullatayn* is not correct, going further to say that it was attributed incorrectly to the Prophet (peace be on him), and these are instead the words of one of the companions. For other examples, see, Ibn Taymiyyah, *Fatāwā*, 21: 512–518, 22: 71–72 and for another example, see, 'Alī b. Muhammad al-Ba'lī, *al-Ikhtiyārāt al-Fiqhiyyah min Fatāwā Shaykh al-Islām Ibn Taymiyyah* (Riyadh: Maktabat al-Riyadh al-Hadīthah, n.d.), 16, [henceforth referred to as "*al-Ikhtiyārāt*"].

[25] Ahmad b. 'Abd al-Halīm Ibn Taymiyyah deals with this issue in various parts of his treatises; see, for instance, his work *Dar' Ta'ārud al-'Aql wa 'l-Naql* (Beirut: Dār al-Kutub al-'Ilmiyyah, 1997).

[26] For some examples of this point, see, Ibn Taymiyyah, *Fatāwā*, 22: 595–596 and 26: 270.

by "weak evidences."[27]

On several occasions, Ibn Taymiyyah's knowledge of *Ḥadīth* helped him to deal with the problem of the existence of conflicting jurisprudential opinions. He asserts that in some cases, all the different opinions have "correct bases," i.e. they are grounded in *Ḥadīth* and therefore all of these opinions are accurate but all of them ought not to be simultaneously acted upon.[28] He perceived differences of opinion on legal issues as instances of legal diversity rather than of conflict.

Moreover, Ibn Taymiyyah's knowledge of the terminology of *Ḥadīth* influenced his legal judgements in several disputes involving jurisprudential specifics. Ibn Taymiyyah asserts that the reason behind these disputes lay in the misunderstanding of some of the complex and ambiguous terminologies related to and found in *Ḥadīth* texts.[29]

With regard to *fiqh*, Ibn Taymiyyah possessed a broad and detailed understanding of the statements and jurisprudential terminology of the eponym of the Ḥanbalī School of law, Aḥmad ibn Ḥanbal (d. 241/855). There are, for instance, several rulings issued by Ḥanbalī scholars which Ibn Taymiyyah has argued to be "incorrect." He attributes this to "the misunderstanding of Aḥmad ibn Ḥanbal's statements and words"[30] and his discussions and clarifications were to have a lasting influence on the subsequent discussions within the school. He does add, however, that at times

---

[27] For instance, in the Ḥanbalī School there is an opinion which states that the recommended prayer before the obligatory *ẓuhr* prayer is four *rak'at*. This opinion is attributed to Aḥmad ibn Ḥanbal and held and mentioned by several leading Ḥanbalī scholars, such as Abū 'l-Khaṭṭāb Maḥfūḍ b. Aḥmad al-Kulwadhānī and Muḥammad b. al-Ḥusayn al-Ājurrī (d. 360/971). This opinion is based on the *ḥadīth* reporting that the Prophet used to pray four *raka'at* before the 'Aṣr prayer. See, 'Alī b. Sulaymān Al-Mardāwī, *al-Inṣāf fī Ma'rifat al-Rājiḥ min al-Khilāf 'alā Madhhab al-Imām Aḥmad ibn Ḥanbal* (Beirut: Mu'assasat al-Ta'rīkh al-'Arabī, n.d.), 2: 177. Ibn Taymiyyah states that this ruling is not accurate as it is based on a weak *ḥadīth*. He asserts that there is no correct *ḥadīth* which supports this ruling. For other examples of this point, see, Ibn Taymiyyah, *Fatāwā*, 21: 512.

[28] Ibn Taymiyyah gives various examples of this point, see for example, his, *Fatāwā*, 22: 335-355.

[29] For example, in the issue of the type of *ḥajj* which was performed by the Prophet (peace be on him), Ibn Taymiyyah attributes the existence of the conflicting opinions in this issue to a number of factors, one of which is the misunderstanding of some terms mentioned in *ḥadīths* dealing with this point. See, Ibn Taymiyyah, *Fatāwā*, 22: 292-293 and 26: 61-79. For further examples of this point, see, ibid., 21: 122.

[30] For examples of this point, see, al-Ba'lī, *al-Ikhtiyārāt*, 54, 76, 211-212. Another point to note is that Ibn Taymiyyah thinks that this problem i.e. the misunderstanding of Aḥmad's words, was not only confined to Ḥanbalī scholars, he points out that even some Imāms, such as Ibn 'Abd al-Barr of the Mālikī School also misunderstood some of Aḥmad's texts. See for example, Ibn Taymiyyah, *Fatāwā*, 22: 589.

Ḥanbalī scholars who did correctly understand the statements and words attributed to Aḥmad, nevertheless failed to correctly apply them to the legal issues under consideration.[31] He further adds that internal discussions in the school were conflated with newly introduced matters that were presumably ascribed to Aḥmad ibn Ḥanbal but on later scrutiny were not entirely accurate[32] and conversely, Ibn Taymiyyah asserts that there are some issues where it is claimed that Aḥmad did not refer to them but the fact was that he did make such reference.[33]

After a scrutiny of Ibn Taymiyyah's discussions of jurisprudential matters it becomes evident that in most cases he would follow a particular method to reach his jurisprudential preferences, or what is known as *al-ikhtiyārāt al-fiqhiyyah*. Ibn Taymiyyah would investigate the various narrations and opinions of his school in a meticulous and comparative manner and would thereafter prefer to a particular opinion.

Ibn Taymiyyah's preferences within Ḥanbalī jurisprudence provided the scholars of his school with the platform upon which they could still be identified as Ḥanbalīs and at the same time adhere to "the most correct opinion" in relation to the various jurisprudential issues. Thus, on account of his extensive knowledge in *Ḥadīth* and *fiqh*, Ibn Taymiyyah was ideally placed to critically examine conflicting reports and / pass judgements on internal conceptual and methodological disputes of the school

Ibn Taymiyyah's opinions with regard to *taqlīd* and *ijtihād* also had a significant impact on his jurisprudential thought. This influence is evident in his position towards the different schools of law.

Ibn Taymiyyah had reservations about having excessive bias towards one particular scholar, stating that it is difficult to argue for one particular scholar as being "the best scholar" because every scholar has strengths where his opinion outweighs those of others.[34] Also, he mentions that any strict preference for a single scholar is no more than a generalisation which is often based on presumption if not mere caprice. This, according to him, leads to contentious disagreements in the Muslim community which is expressly forbidden in Islam.[35]

Instead of such preference between scholars, Ibn Taymiyyah insists upon tolerance between the various schools of law. He cites the example of the Prophet's Companions who accepted different views, declaring that the

---

[31] See, for instance, ibid., 23: 280.

[32] See, for instance, ibid., 23: 278.

[33] See for instance, ibid., 21: 179, 300, 407, and 22: 588–590, 621, 622, and 25: 241.

[34] Ibid., 22: 293.

[35] See, ibid., 22: 291–292.

various parties would be rewarded for their independent reasoning.[36] Therefore, Ibn Taymiyyah concludes, the same principle must be applied to the opinions of other scholars. Those who prefer to imitate al-Shāfiʿī, for instance, should not disapprove of those who prefer to follow Aḥmad ibn Ḥanbal and *vice versa*.[37] He asserts that no one can impose the opinions of his school on others.[38] Furthermore, he insists that partial conversion from one school of law to another in some situations is even obligatory. For instance, if the imitator (*muqallid*) knows that certain opinions in his school are in opposition to clear texts and that correct opinions are held by another school of law, he must follow what is correct even though it is not from his own school.[39]

Similarly, Ibn Taymiyyah asserts that the existence of these "incorrect opinions" in a school of law should not be used as an excuse to attack those scholars. As he explains, this is because those scholars were *mujtahids*. In reality, however, these scholars were targets of strong attacks from lay people and even some scholars. In an attempt to counter this antagonism, Ibn Taymiyyah composed *Rafʿ al-Malām* in which he defends the *mujtahid* scholars and clarifies the reasons underlying their rulings which were thought to be in opposition to the texts. Ibn Taymiyyah argues that the leading scholars did not deliberately intend to oppose the *sunnah* of the Prophet (peace be on him) in any manner. It is clear that he is limiting his assertion to those scholars whom he describes as "generally accepted by the Muslim *ummah*."[40] He justifies his assertion in arguing further that the leading scholars did not deliberately oppose the *sunnah* of the Prophet (peace be on him) by the fact that "they are in definite agreement on the obligation of following the Prophet (peace be on him), while it is allowed that the words of anyone other than the Prophet can [either] be accepted or rejected."[41]

In his attempt to absolve a *mujtahid* from any blame of contravening direct textual evidences, Ibn Taymiyyah proposes three most likely reasons which lead to disagreement and at times even conflict among jurists: the first rests upon the *mujtahid's* belief in the non-existence of a *ḥadīth* text cited as evidence by his opponent. The second is that the *mujtahid* may have thought that the implication of the *ḥadīth* (textual or otherwise) had no connection

---

[36] See, ibid., 22: 292–293.

[37] Ibid.

[38] Ibid., 27: 300.

[39] See, ibid., 27: 210–216. Cf. also, al-Matroudi, *The Hanbali School of Law*, 84–9.

[40] Aḥmad b. ʿAbd al-Ḥalim Ibn Taymiyyah, *Rafʿ al-Malām ʿan al-Aʾimmat al-Aʿlām* (Riyadh: al-Riʾāsah al-ʿĀmmah li Idārāt al-Buḥūth al-ʿIlmiyyah, 1413 AH), 8.

[41] Ibid., 9.

with that aspect of the question that he was investigating. Finally, the *mujtahid* may have thought that the ruling contained in the *ḥadīth* had actually been abrogated.[42]

Ibn Taymiyyah argues that the first reason for the conflict can exist in several ways. Firstly, it may have been the case that the scholar had no knowledge of the *ḥadīth* text. According to Ibn Taymiyyah, this is the predominant reason for the divergence between the text and the ruling derived by a *mujtahid*. This, as he explains, is because of the vastness of the *Sunnah*. Ibn Taymiyyah does not think that this reason was confined to the era before the canonical collections of *Ḥadīth* as these collections do not contain all of the *Sunnah*. Moreover, it is difficult for every scholar to know all the *ḥadīths* contained within these canonical collections, for their number is very large.[43]

Secondly, a scholar may believe that the *ḥadīth* that was cited was not actually uttered by the Prophet (peace be on him) because the *mujtahid* had received the *ḥadīth* through an unreliable chain of transmission (*isnād*). This second case, as Ibn Taymiyyah observes, existed more widely after the first generation of Islam, because during the first century there was no need for studying chains of transmitters contrary to the successive generations where the need for caution and rigorous evaluative methods were required owing to extensive fabrication of the *ḥadīths*.[44] Thirdly, it is possible that the *ḥadīth* was known to the *mujtahid* but he did not base his ruling on it either because he forgot the *ḥadīth* itself or did not consider it to be relevant.[45]

The second cause of disagreement, according to Ibn Taymiyyah, is that the *mujtahid* may have failed to know the indications of the text relevant for the ruling. This may be because of the existence of some "strange" and anomalous (*gharīb*) words or complex and ambiguous terms in that text which prevented the *mujtahid* from comprehending the intended meaning. It may also be due to the fact that the *mujtahid* might have concluded that there is in fact no indication that exists in the text relevant for the corresponding ruling.[46]

The difference between this last point and the previous one, as Ibn Taymiyyah explains, is that in the latter case the scholar did not extract the ruling on this text because of his understanding and his application of the principles of jurisprudence, whereas in the former case what prevented the scholar from implementing the relevant text is his failure to grasp the full

---

[42] See, ibid.

[43] See, ibid., 9-18.

[44] See, ibid., 18-19.

[45] See, ibid., 22-25.

[46] See, ibid., 25-29.

implication of the text required for an informed extraction of a ruling.[47]

The third and final cause for conflict, according to Ibn Taymiyyah, is that the *mujtahid* did not act upon a *ḥadīth* text because it was in conflict with something that led him to believe in its weakness or that he thought that the ruling it contained had been abrogated.[48]

Ibn Taymiyyah is aware that a *mujtahid* unquestionably has the right to apply his legal principles (*uṣūl*) whereby all legal texts are cumulatively understood and assessed within a dynamic framework of interpretation and analysis as opposed to a static approach of merely taking the *ḥadīth* text *prima facie* without any other consideration. This constitutes an additional cause for a *ḥadīth* text to be discarded in favour of methodological principles. The additional factors that Ibn Taymiyyah mentions are, firstly, that one *mujtahid* may discard the *ḥadīth* cited as evidence by another *mujtahid* on the consideration of the locality of transmitters within the corresponding *isnād*. Thus, some scholars from Ḥijāz reject transmitters or narrations from parts of 'Irāq or Shām as legitimate evidence unless they initially originated from Ḥijāz. Ibn Taymiyyah comments that "most people, however, do not use this as a basis for deeming such a *ḥadīth* as weak (*ḍaʿīf*). So whenever the chain of transmitters is sound, the *ḥadīth* is authoritative, regardless of whether it is Ḥijāzī, 'Irāqī, Shāmī or from other regions."[49]

The second additional cause of disagreement is generated by the different conditions stipulated by different scholars for the acceptance of the singular reported *ḥadīth* (*khabar al-wāḥid*).[50]

The third additional factor for creating conflict is what Ibn Taymiyyah characterises as "perceived consensuses." He defines this form of consensus as "not being aware of any dissenting view." This, according to Ibn Taymiyyah, led to the reluctance of some scholars in following some of the textual proofs due to the fear of opposing this "perceived consensus."[51]

More importantly, Ibn Taymiyyah deals in *Rafʿ al-Malām* with the result of *ijtihād* and its link to the promise of a reward or the threat of a punishment. He asserts that even when there exist good reasons to necessitate that a person deserved that the threat of punishment be applied, it might still not come about due to the existence of a legal or justifiable impediment (*māniʿ*), and there are various types of impediments which he regards as unlikely to be lacking as far as the *mukallaf* is concerned, such as repentance (*tawbah*), asking

---

[47] See, ibid., 29.

[48] See, ibid., 31.

[49] Ibid., 21-22.

[50] See, ibid., 22.

[51] See, ibid., 31-33.

for forgiveness (*istighfār*), good deeds that erase sins (*al-ḥasanāt al-māḥiyah li 'l-sayyi'āt*), tribulations (*balā' al-dunyā*) and calamities (*maṣā'ib*).[52]

Ibn Taymiyyah argues that the function of a threat is to clarify that the deed associated with the threat is a reason for the punishment mentioned in the threat and therefore the prohibition of that deed and its reprehensible nature could be inferred from the threat. However, he thinks that it is not justified to conclude that if the reason for the threat was to be found in someone, then this would necessitate the occurrence of its effect which is the punishment. He relates this to the fact that the effect depends on the existence of its conditions and the removal of all of its impediments.[53]

These opinions of Ibn Taymiyyah regarding the issues of *ijtihād*, *taqlīd* and jurisprudential disputes (*ikhtilāf*) have undoubtedly influenced his understanding of Islamic law as well as his relation with the Ḥanbalī school and other schools. This can be seen clearly from his use of independent reasoning and his "corrections" of various rules and rulings within these schools, especially the Ḥanbalī school. Also, these opinions led to Ibn Taymiyyah's readiness to acknowledge his own mistakes[54] and to have a forgiving attitude towards his opponents.[55] It is likely that this consideration and sensitivity stems from the fact that Ibn Taymiyyah had studied under a great number of scholars who belonged to various schools and thus acquired a diverse legal training and education.[56] This cumulative experience, no doubt, shaped Ibn Taymiyyah's legacy on Islamic law, one which calls for more intellectual tolerance among jurists and one which is clearly manifest from the following text.

Rafʿ al-Malām should, however be read in the context of the time in which Ibn Taymiyyah lived. This was an era of staunch *taqlīd* in which entrenched allegiances and affiliations and even a degree of fanaticism were quite widespread, not only among the lay public but also in the circles of the learned.

■ ■ ■

---

[52] See, ibid., 42.

[53] See, ibid.

[54] See, for instance, al-Baʿlī, *al-Ikhtiyārāt*, 16, 22, 23–24, 107, 121; Ibn Taymiyyah, *Fatāwā*, 21: 512–518 and 22: 71–72.

[55] See, al-Karmī, *al-Kawākib*, 139, 174.

[56] See, Henri Laoust, *Naẓariyyāt Shaykh al-Islām Ibn Taymiyyah fī al-Siyāsah wa 'l-Ijtimāʿ* (Cairo: Dār al-Anṣār, 1977), 204.

II

TRANSLATION

of

Raf' al-Malām 'an al-A'immat al-A'lām

In the Name of Allah, the Beneficent, the Merciful

Praise is due to Allah for His bounties. I testify that there is no deity except Him; He has no associates in the heavens and the earth. And I testify that Muḥammad is His slave and Messenger[57] and the seal of His Prophets—peace be on him and his family and Companions, continuous prayers and blessings until we meet him.

To proceed:

It is obligatory upon Muslims, after being loyal to Allah the Exalted and His Messenger (peace be on him), to be loyal to the believers, as the Qur'ān declares, especially to the scholars who are the inheritors of the Prophets (peace be on them], whom Allah made like stars that serve as guides through the darkness of the land and the oceans. The Muslims are in agreement as regards their guidance and understanding. For prior to the advent of our Prophet Muḥammad (peace be on him), the scholars of the earlier [Prophets'] communities were less inclined to good, whereas the scholars of the Muslim community (*ummah*) were deemed to be the finest as they carried the mantle of knowledge bequeathed by the Prophet (peace be on him) and they are the revivers of whatever was forgotten of his *Sunnah*. Through them the Qur'ān is established, and they act upon it; the Qur'ān speaks through them, and they articulate whatever the Qur'ān contains.

It should be known that none of the Imāms who are generally accepted by the Muslim *ummah* would intentionally oppose the Prophet (peace be on

---

[57] It should be indicated that the two terms (*al-Nabī* and *al-Rasūl*), have been both rendered into English as "Prophet" due to the fact that in *Raf' al-Malām* the author uses them interchangeably as in most cases in the text they are both used in association with the Prophet Muḥammad (peace be on him) and therefore the discussion regarding the difference between *al-nabī* and *al-rasūl* among theologians would not arise in this case. Also, the term (*al-kitāb*) referring to the Qur'ān has been rendered into English as the Qur'ān rather than 'the Book' as the latter might lead to confusion especially if the reader is not aware of such technical terminologies.

him) in any aspect of his *Sunnah,* whether small or great. This is because they are in profound agreement regarding the obligation of following the Prophet (peace be on him).[58] They believe that the words of anyone other than the Prophet (peace be on him) may be accepted or rejected. If any of their opinions was found to be in opposition to an authentic *ḥadīth,* then there must be a just excuse for that and these excuses fall under one of the three categories:

Firstly, that the scholar did not believe that the Prophet (peace be on him) [actually] uttered the *ḥadīth.*

Secondly, that the scholar did not think that the issue in question was [actually] intended to be covered by the Prophetic *ḥadīth.*

Thirdly, that the scholar believed the ruling [contained in the *ḥadīth*] to have been abrogated.

These three categories can be further divided into a number of more specific reasons:

The first reason: that the *ḥadīth* did not reach the concerned scholar; and whoever is not aware of a *ḥadīth,* is not held responsible for not knowing its ruling. Thus, if the *ḥadīth* did not reach him and he gave a judgement regarding a particular question on the basis of the apparent meaning of a verse or another *ḥadīth* or on the basis of analogy or the presumption of continuity (*istiṣḥāb*), then his opinion might fortuitously agree with the *ḥadīth* in one case while opposing it on another.

This is the most likely reason for most of what is found in the opinions of the Pious Predecessors (*al-salaf al-ṣāliḥ*) that oppose certain *ḥadīth*s. Indeed, it is simply not possible for any single member of the *ummah* to know all the *ḥadīth*s of the Prophet (peace be on him). The Prophet (peace be on him) used to speak, issue legal verdicts (*fatāwā*), pass judgement, or perform an action which was heard or seen by those who were present at the time and they, or some of them, would convey it to others who would in turn convey it to others until it would reach whomever Allah (the Most High) willed among the scholars from amongst the Companions of the Prophet, their Followers and those who came after them.

And in another assembly, such matters would be heard or seen by those who were absent from the first gathering and they [too] would convey it to whomever they were able to. As a result, the first group would know what was not known by the other and *vice versa* and so the scholars among the

---

[58] See, Muḥammad b. Idrīs al-Shāfiʿī, *al-Risālah* (Cairo: Maṭbaʿat al-Ḥalabī, 1939), 74, 104.

Companions and those who came after them would surpass each other in the relative levels of the extent of their knowledge or the quality of it.

[As we have said], it is absolutely impossible to claim that any one person could encompass all of the *hadīths* of the Prophet (peace be on him) and this can be illustrated through the example of the Righteous Caliphs, who were most knowledgeable regarding the affairs of the Prophet (peace be on him), his *Sunnah* and other matters relating to him, especially [Abū Bakr] al-Ṣiddīq (may Allah be pleased with him), who was never far from the Prophet whether at home or on his travels. In fact he was with him most of the time to the extent that he used to stay with him at night to deal with the Muslims' affairs.[59] This is also true of 'Umar b. al-Khaṭṭāb (may Allah be pleased with him) and you will find many *hadīths* in which the Prophet (peace be on him) said, "I entered with Abū Bakr and 'Umar" and "I went out with Abū Bakr and 'Umar."[60] Despite this, when Abū Bakr (may Allah be pleased with him) was asked about the grandmother's share of inheritance, he replied, "There is nothing prescribed for you in Allah's Book, nor do I know anything for you in the *Sunnah* of the Prophet of Allah (peace be on him), but I will ask people [about it]." So he did ask them and al-Mughīrah b. Shu'bah and Muḥammad b. Maslamah came forward and testified that the Prophet (peace be on him) had given her a sixth.[61] This *sunnah* was also reported by 'Imrān b. Ḥuṣayn.[62] Thus, even though none of these three Companions was of the same stature as Abū Bakr and the other caliphs, they were the only ones who knew this particular *sunnah* about whose practice the *ummah* has since agreed upon.[63]

Similarly, 'Umar b. al-Khaṭṭāb (may Allah be pleased with him) did not know the *sunnah* relating to "seeking permission" (*isti'dhān*) [before entering a

---

[59] Aḥmad b. Muḥammad al-Ṭaḥāwī, *Sharḥ Maʿānī 'l-Āthār* (Beirut: Dār al-Kutub al-'Ilmiyyah, 1399 AH), 4: 330.

[60] See for instance, Muḥammad b. Ismā'īl al-Bukhārī, *Ṣaḥīḥ al-Bukhārī* [henceforth referred to as "*Ṣaḥīḥ*"], Kitāb al-Ṣulḥ, Bāb al-Ṣulḥ bayn al-Ghuramā' and Kitāb Faḍā'il al-Ṣaḥābah, Bāb Manāqib 'Umar, as well as the testimony of the caliph 'Alī regarding this in al-Bukhārī, *Ṣaḥīḥ*, Kitāb Faḍā'il al-Ṣaḥābah, Bāb Manāqib 'Umar.

[61] Muḥammad b. 'Īsā al-Tirmidhī, *al-Jāmi' al-Mukhtaṣar min al-Sunan* [henceforth referred to as "*Sunan*"], Kitāb al-Farā'iḍ, Bāb mā Jā' fī Mīrāth al-Jaddah; Muḥammad b. Yazīd Ibn Mājah, *Sunan Ibn Mājah*, Kitāb al-Farā'iḍ, Bāb Mīrāth al-Jaddah.

[62] See, for a discussion about the authenticity of these reports, Muḥammad b. 'Alī al-Shawkānī, *Nayl al-Awṭār min Aḥādīth Sayyid al-Akhyār Sharḥ Muntaqā 'l-Akhbār* (Beirut: Dār al-Jīl, 1973), 6: 175–177.

[63] See for the discussion about the share of the grandmother, 'Abd Allāh b. Aḥmad Ibn Qudāmah, *al-Mughnī fī Fiqh al-Imām Aḥmad b. Ḥanbal al-Shaybānī* (Beirut: Dār al-Fikr, 1405 AH), 6: 189; Muḥammad b. Aḥmad Ibn Rushd, *Bidāyat al-Mujtahid wa Nihāyat al-Muqtaṣid* (Beirut: Dār al-Fikr, n.d.), 2: 262–263 for.

dwelling] until he was informed about it by Abū Mūsā al-Ash'arī who cited the Anṣār in support of his narration,[64] and this is while 'Umar was more knowledgeable than the one who related this *sunnah* to him. Likewise, 'Umar did not know that the wife inherits from the blood money of her deceased husband. Instead, he thought that the blood money belonged to the *'āqilah*[65] until al-Ḍaḥḥāk ibn Sufyān al-Kilābī, who was appointed by the Prophet (peace be on him) as a governor of certain regions, wrote to 'Umar informing him that the Prophet (peace be on him) gave the wife of Ashyam al-Ḍibābī (may Allah be pleased with him) [a share] of her deceased husband's blood money. As a result, 'Umar abandoned his opinion in favour of this *ḥadīth* and said: "If I had not heard this *ḥadīth*, I would have judged contrary to it."[66]

'Umar also did not know the ruling of *jizyah* for the Magians [followers of a fire-worshipping religion] until he was informed by 'Abd al-Raḥmān b. 'Awf (may Allah be pleased with him) that the Prophet (peace be on him) said, "Treat them as you treat the People of the Book."[67] Moreover, when 'Umar reached Sargh [near Tabūk] and was informed that a plague had stricken al-Shām [the region of greater Syria], he consulted the early Muhājirūn[68] who were with him at the time. He then asked the Anṣār,[69] then he asked those who accepted Islam at the time of the conquest of Makkah, and every one of them told him what they thought and none of them was able to inform him of a *sunnah* from the Prophet (peace be on him) until 'Abd al-Raḥmān b. 'Awf came and told him of the *sunnah* of the Prophet (peace be on him) with regard to plagues, when he said: "If the plague appears in a land while you are in it,

---

[64] See, al-Bukhārī, *Ṣaḥīḥ*, Kitāb al-Isti'dhān, Bāb al-Taslīm wa 'l-Isti'dhān Thalāthan; Muslim b. al-Ḥajjāj al-Naysābūrī [henceforth referred to as "Muslim"], *Ṣaḥīḥ Muslim* [henceforth referred to as "*Ṣaḥīḥ*"], Kitāb al-Ādāb, Bāb al-Isti'dhān.

[65] There is a discussion about who is meant by *'āqilah* in Islamic law. One of the opinions is that it is the paternal uncles and their children, however distant they are in descent. Another opinion states that *'āqilah* includes the father, sons, brothers and every agnatic heir. Ibn Taymiyyah holds a different opinion from these two. He asserts that *'āqilah* is "every individual who helps and supports the person at the time and the place." See, al-Matroudi, *The Hanbali School of Law*, 118–119.

[66] See, Mālik b. Anas al-Aṣbuḥī, *Muwaṭṭa' al-Imām Mālik* (Egypt: Dār Iḥyā' al-Turāth, n.d.), 2: 866; Aḥmad b. Muḥammad b. Ḥanbal, *Musnad al-Imām Aḥmad b. Ḥanbal* (Cairo: Mu'assasat Qurṭubah, n.d.), 3: 452 and Sulaymān b. al-Ash'ath Abū Dāwūd al-Sijistānī, *Sunan Abī Dāwūd*, Kitāb al-Farā'iḍ, Bāb fī 'l-Mar'ah Tarith min Diyat Zawjihā.

[67] See, Mālik, *Muwaṭṭa'*, 1: 278; also see, 'Abd Allāh b. Yūsuf al-Zayla'ī, *Naṣb al-Rāyah li Aḥādīth al-Hidāyah* (Cairo: Dār al-Ḥadīth, 1357), 3: 448–449 and Muḥammad b. Aḥmad Ibn 'Abd al-Hādī, *Tanqīḥ Taḥqīq Aḥādīth al-Ta'līq* (Beirut: Dār al-Kutub al-'Ilmiyyah, 1998), 3: 364.

[68] The emigrants from Makkah to Madīnah.

[69] The Madīnan followers of the Prophet (peace be on him) who granted him refuge after the *hijrah* to Madīnah.

do not depart in flight from it and if you hear that it has smitten a land, do not go towards it."[70]

On another occasion, 'Umar discussed with Ibn 'Abbās (may Allah be pleased with both of them) the problem of one who has experienced doubts concerning his prayer [i.e. whether he had missed an element of it or not] and 'Umar was not aware of any *sunnah* pertaining to this matter. He was then informed by 'Abd al-Raḥmān b. 'Awf that the Prophet (peace be on him) said that "the one performing the prayer should ignore his doubt and base his action on whatever is certain to him."[71] Finally, 'Umar was once travelling on a particularly windy day. He asked: "Who can tell us [from the Prophet] something with regard to the wind?" Abū Hurayrah (may Allah be pleased with him) said: "I was informed of 'Umar's request while I was at the back of the group so I spurred my riding camel to hasten forward until I reached him and narrated to him what the Prophet (peace be on him) ordered when the wind would rage."[72]

Thus, these were the issues that were not known to 'Umar until he was informed about them by those who were not his equal in rank. Indeed, there were other issues in which 'Umar knew nothing from the *sunnah* as a result of which he pronounced a judgement, or issued a *fatwā* on them in a way that might not have been in [direct] conformity with the *Sunnah*. An example of this is his judgement on the blood money for fingers, namely that they are different from one another based on their different functions, whereas both Abū Mūsā and Ibn 'Abbās (may Allah be pleased with them), both of whom were lesser in degree of knowledge than 'Umar, knew the Prophet's saying, "This and this are equal,"[73] meaning the thumb and little finger. This *sunnah* reached Mu'āwiyah (may Allah be pleased with him) during the time of his rule, and he judged in accordance with it and the Muslims felt that it was incumbent upon them to follow it. The fact that 'Umar was not aware of this *ḥadīth* was not considered a shortcoming on his part.

Another example is 'Umar and his son 'Abd Allāh (may Allah be pleased with both of them) as well as other notable scholars prohibiting the wearing of perfume by the one who is about to enter into a state of ritual consecration (*iḥrām*) and by the one who is about to go to Makkah for circumambulation

---

[70] See, al-Bukhārī, *Ṣaḥīḥ*, Kitāb al-Ṭibb, Bāb man Kharaja min Arḍ lā Tulāyimuh; Muslim, *Ṣaḥīḥ*, Kitāb al-Salām, Bāb al-Ṭā'ūn.

[71] For the *ḥadīths* attributed to 'Abd al-Raḥmān ibn 'Awf regarding this, see, Muḥammad b. Jarīr al-Ṭabarī, *Tahdhīb al-Āthār* (Damascus: Dār al-Ma'mūn li 1-Turāth, 1995), 33.

[72] See Aḥmad, *Musnad*, 2: 267 and 'Abd al-Razzāq b. Hammām al-Ṣan'ānī, *al-Muṣannaf* (Beirut: al-Maktab al-Islāmī, 1403 AH), 11: 89.

[73] See al-Bukhārī, *Ṣaḥīḥ*, Kitāb al-Diyāt, Bāb idhā 'Aḍḍa Rajulan fa Waqa'at Thanāyāh.

of the Ka'bah (*tawāf*) after throwing the stones at Jamarat al-'Aqabah, not being aware of the *hadīth* of 'Ā'ishah (may Allah be pleased with her) in which she said: "I perfumed the Prophet (peace be on him) for his *ihrām* before he entered into the state of *ihrām*, and I also perfumed him before performing the *hajj* circumambulation (*tawāf al-ifādah*) (i.e. after the first state of *ihrām* elapses)."[74]

'Umar used to allow the one who wears leather socks to wipe over them until he takes them off without any restriction [as to time]. This was adhered to by a group of the early pious predecessors because the *hadīth* regarding the time restriction on wiping that was authenticated by some of those who were not their equal in knowledge had not reached them.[75] This *hadīth* was narrated from the Prophet (peace be on him) through various authentic channels of transmission.[76]

The same holds for 'Uthmān (may Allah be pleased with him) who did not know that a woman should spend the waiting period following the death of her husband in the house where she lived before his death, until al-Furay'ah bint Mālik—Abū Sa'īd al-Khudrī's sister (may Allah be pleased with both of them)—related to him that when her husband passed away the Prophet (peace be on him) told her "Remain in your house until you fulfil the period stated in the Qur'ān for this matter [four months and ten days]." 'Uthmān (may Allah be pleased with him) then acted upon this *hadīth*.[77]

He was also once given meat [i.e. while he was in a state of *ihrām*] from a hunt which was hunted specially for him as a gift and upon sitting down to eat it 'Alī (may Allah be pleased with him) informed him that the Prophet (peace be on him) rejected the meat [from a hunt] given to him as a present."[78]

And likewise 'Alī (may Allah be pleased with him) who said: "When I used to hear a *hadīth* from the Messenger of Allah (peace be on him), directly Allah made me benefit from all that He desired me to benefit from, whereas if anyone else would relate something to me, I would make him swear an oath and if he did, I would believe him. Abū Bakr told me—and he was being truthful—and he mentioned the well-known *hadīth* related to the Prayer of Repentance (*salāt al-tawbah*).[79]

---

⁷⁴ See, al-Bukhārī, *Sahīh*, Kitāb al-Hajj, Bāb al-Tīb 'ind al-Ihrām; Muslim, *Sahīh*, Kitāb al-Hajj, Bāb al-Tīb li 'l-Muhrim 'ind al-Ihrām.

⁷⁵ See, Yahyā b. Sharaf al-Nawāwī, *Sahīh Muslim bi Sharh al-Nawāwī* (Beirut: Dār Ihyā' al-Turāth, 1392), 3: 176.

⁷⁶ See for example, Muslim, *Sahīh*, Kitāb al-Tahārah, Bāb al-Tawqīt fī 'l-Mash.

⁷⁷ See, Abū Dāwūd, *Sunan*, Kitāb al-Talāq, Bāb fī 'l-Mutawaffā 'Anhā.

⁷⁸ See, Ahmad, *Musnad*, 1: 100.

⁷⁹ See, Abū Dāwūd, *Sunan*, Kitāb al-Salāh, Bāb fī 'l-Istighfār; Ibn Mājah, *Sunan*, Kitāb Iqāmat al-

'Alī and Ibn 'Abbās (may Allah be pleased with them), among others, issued a *fatwā* that the woman whose husband died while she was pregnant, must observe the longer of the two specified waiting periods. The *sunnah* of the Messenger of Allah (peace be on him) regarding Subay'ah al-Aslamiyyah (may Allah be pleased with her) had not reached them. Upon the death of her husband Sa'd b. Khawlah, the Prophet (peace be on him) told her that her waiting period continues to the point of the child's delivery.[80]

Finally, 'Alī, Zayd, Ibn 'Umar and others (may Allah be pleased with them all) issued a *fatwā* regarding the woman who authorizes her husband to determine her dower (*al-mufawwiḍah*) that, "if her husband passes away, she is not entitled to any dower." The *sunnah* of the Messenger of Allah (peace be on him) pertaining to Barwa' bint Wāshiq (may Allah be pleased with her) had however not reached them.[81]

This is a vast subject area in which a tremendous amount of narrations is related from the Companions of the Prophet (peace be on him). As for that which is related from those other than the Companions it runs into the thousands. This was the position with regard to the Companions who were the most knowledgeable, the most grounded in jurisprudence, the most mindful of Allah and the best among the Muslim community. As for those who came after them, they are lesser in rank and it goes without saying that some of the corpus of the *Sunnah* was hidden from each and every one of them. Therefore, whoever believes that every authentic *ḥadīth* reached each and every one of the Imāms or indeed any one specific Imām, commits a grave and abhorrent error.

It should not be said that the *ḥadīth*s have all been documented and compiled and therefore it is unlikely that they would have been unknown. This is because the well-known collections of *Ḥadīth* were compiled after the demise of the Imāms who are followed (may Allah have mercy on them all). Also, it is not acceptable to claim that the *ḥadīth*s of the Prophet (peace be on him) are limited to those found in the specific collections of *Ḥadīth*. Moreover, even if this were to be the case, not everything in these collections would be known by a single scholar, and this is highly unlikely to be the case with any

---

Ṣalāh, Bāb mā Jā' fī ann al-Ṣalāt Kaffārah; al-Tirmidhī, *Sunan*, Kitāb Abwāb al-Ṣalāh, Bāb mā Jā' fī 'l-Ṣalāt 'ind al-Tawbah; Aḥmad, *Musnad*, 1: 2.

[80] See, al-Bukhārī, *Ṣaḥīḥ*, Kitāb al-Tafsīr, Bāb wa Ūlāt al-Aḥmāl; Muslim, *Ṣaḥīḥ*, Kitāb al-Ṭalāq, Bāb Inqiḍā' al-'Iddah.

[81] See, Abū Dāwūd, *Sunan*, Kitāb al-Nikāḥ, Bāb fī man Tazawwaja wa lam Yusami Ṣidāqan ḥattā Māt; Ibn Mājah, *Sunan*, Kitāb al-Nikāḥ, Bāb al-Rajul Yatazawwaj wa lā Yafriḍ lahā; al-Tirmidhī, *Sunan*, Kitāb al-Nikāḥ, Bāb mā Jā' fī 'l-Rajul Yatazawwaj al-Mara'ah fa Yamūt 'Anhā qabla an Yafriḍ lahā. The ruling according to these narrations is that the widow will be granted her full dower.

person; indeed it is possible that a scholar might possess a large number of collections of *Ḥadīth* and yet not be aware of all of the *ḥadīth*s contained within them. In fact, those who came before the emergence of these *Ḥadīth* collections were by far more knowledgeable in the *Sunnah* than those who came after them. This is because a large part of the *Sunnah* that had reached them and had been authenticated by them might not have reached us except through unknown transmitters or a severed chain of narration or might not have reached us at all. Thus, it can be said that their "*Ḥadīth* compilations" were preserved in their hearts, which contained several times as much as that which is found in the physical collections and the one who is well versed in this issue will have no doubts about this [point].

Nor should it be said that whoever does not have knowledge of all of the *ḥadīth*s should not be considered a *mujtahid*. This is because if we were to stipulate as a condition of the *mujtahid* that he must be aware of all of the Prophet's words and actions relevant to legal rulings then there would not be a single *mujtahid* in the Muslim community. Rather, the *mujtahid*'s objective should be to know most of the *ḥadīth*s so that only a few of the details will escape him and hence he might only contradict the few details that had [not][82] reached him.

The second reason: that the *ḥadīth* had reached the *mujtahid* but its authenticity, in his opinion, was not established. This may be because the [direct] transmitter of the *ḥadīth* to him or the one before him or any one of the transmitters in that *ḥadīth*'s chain of transmission is considered by him to be unknown [or unidentifiable], or of doubtful reputation (*muttaham*), or deficient in memory. It may also be because the *ḥadīth* did not reach the *mujtahid* with a continuous chain but rather with a severed chain of transmitters, or that the transmitter was not precise when transmitting the wording of the *ḥadīth* even though the same *ḥadīth* was transmitted to other scholars by trustworthy transmitters with an uninterrupted *isnād*. This might be because the one whom the *mujtahid* considered unknown was known by others to be trustworthy or that it was narrated by other than those whom he considered to be impugned authorities (*majrūḥūn*), or that the *ḥadīth* was narrated through another uninterrupted chain, or that some of the memorizers among scholars of *Ḥadīth* narrated the wording of the *ḥadīth* meticulously, or that there were *shawāhid* [i.e. other Companions transmitting supporting narrations] and *mutāba'āt* [i.e. the *ḥadīth* being narrated by another chain of transmitters reaching back to one of the transmitters after the Companion] indicating the authenticity of that narration.

---

[82] The word (not) is missing from the printed text of all available published editions of *Raf' al-Malām 'an al-A'immat al-A'lām.*

This [second reason] was also very common at the time of the first generation of Successors (*tābiʿīn*) and the second generation of Successors (*tābiʿī 'l-tābiʿīn*) up to the time of the well known Imāms, more so than the first generation. Indeed, it is more common than the first reason. *Ḥadīths* were widespread by then and well known but they reached many of the scholars through weak channels, even though they had reached others through comparatively authentic channels. Therefore, they were considered to be an authoritative source (*ḥujjah*) because they were transmitted through these authentic channels, and yet they were not known to those who opposed them because of the weak transmissions available to them. This is why we find that many scholars suspended judgement on account of a *ḥadīth* until its authenticity was properly established, so they would say: "my opinion in this issue is such and such. However, if there is a *ḥadīth* narrated with regard to this [containing another ruling], and if its authenticity was to be established, then my ruling would be in accordance with it."[83]

The third reason: that the *ḥadīth* was deemed to be weak on the basis of the *ijtihād* of one scholar while others disagreed with him, regardless of whether the narration of the *ḥadīth* arrived through another channel or whether the correct opinion was that of this *mujtahid*, his opponents, or both of them, according to those who say that "every *mujtahid* is correct."

There can be various causes for this:

One of them is that one scholar believes that a transmitter of the concerned *ḥadīth* is weak whereas the other believes him/her to be trustworthy. And the science related to identifying transmitters is a vast one. It is possible that the correct *mujtahid* is the one who believes that the transmitter is weak, because he was aware of an impugning factor. Also, it is possible that the correct opinion is with the other *mujtahid* because he knew that the cause was not an impugning factor, either because it did not actually fall into a valid class of impugning factors or that the transmitter had an exemption which precludes the effect of the impugnment upon him.

This is another vast subject area and the scholars specialising in the transmitters and their conditions [i.e. the study of the reporters of *Ḥadīth*] have their agreements and disagreements with regard to this issue, just as the scholars specialising in all of the other sciences do.

Another reason is that the *mujtahid* does not believe that the transmitter heard the *ḥadīth* from the narrator on the authority of whom he is transmitting it whereas another *mujtahid* believes that the transmitter did

---

[83] Muḥammad b. Aḥmad al-Dhahabī, *Siyar Aʿlām al-Nubalāʾ* (Beirut: Muʾassasat al-Risālah, 1413 AH), 10: 35 and ʿAlī b. al-Ḥasan ibn Hibat Allāh Ibn ʿAsākir, *Taʾrīkh Madīnat Dimashq wa Dhikr Faḍlihā wa Tasmiyat man Ḥallahā min al-Amāthil* (Beirut: Dār al-Fikr, 1995), 51: 389.

indeed hear the *ḥadīth* [from the narrator on the authority of whom he is transmitting it]. And the causes bringing this about are well-known.

Yet another reason is that the transmitter has two states: a state of soundness and a state of confusion (*iḍṭirāb*), e.g. when a transmitter becomes confused or when his books are burnt down. Therefore, all that he transmitted while in a sound state is [considered] correct and all that he transmitted while in a state of confusion is [considered] weak. As a result, it might not appear clear to one *mujtahid* as regards the state in which the *ḥadīth* was transmitted whereas another *mujtahid* was certain that the transmitter related that *ḥadīth* while in his sound state.

Another reason is that the transmitter forgets that he related the *ḥadīth* and is hence unable to remember it at a later date or he actually denies that he ever related the *ḥadīth*. Hence, one *mujtahid* might believe that this is a defect necessitating the abandonment of the *ḥadīth* whereas another *mujtahid* might believe that it is acceptable to cite that *ḥadīth* as evidence—and this topic of dispute [too] is well-known.

A further reason is that many of the Ḥijāzī scholars hold the view that the ʿIrāqī or Shāmī *ḥadīth* should not be cited as an evidence unless it originated in Ḥijāz, to the point where some of them remarked: "Give the *ḥadīth*s of the people of ʿIrāq the same status as the narrations of the People of the Book; neither affirm them nor disbelieve them." And another [Ḥijāzī] was asked: "Is the following chain of transmission authoritative: Sufyān from Manṣūr from Ibrāhīm from ʿAlqamah on the authority of ʿAbd Allāh b. Masʿūd?" The reply was: "If it did not originate in Ḥijāz, then no."

This is due to the fact that they believed that the people of Ḥijāz had mastered the *Sunnah*, so that none of it had escaped them, whereas there was confusion regarding the *ḥadīth*s of ʿIrāq which necessitated a suspension of judgement on them. Some of the ʿIrāqīs, on the other hand, think the same about the *ḥadīth* of the people of Shām. Most people, however, do not use this as a basis for weakening a *ḥadīth*. So whenever the chain of transmitters is sound, the *ḥadīth* is authoritative, whether it is Ḥijāzī, ʿIrāqī, Shāmī or from other places. Abū Dāwūd al-Sijistānī (may Allah have mercy upon him) compiled a book on the narrations of *ḥadīth*s known to be related only by individuals from certain regions (*mafārīd*), in which he clarified those *ḥadīth*s which could only be found with continuous chains of transmission in those particular regions and not in other regions. This includes *ḥadīth*s from Madīnah, Makkah, Ṭāʾif, Dimashq, Ḥimṣ, Kūfah, Baṣrah and others. There are reasons other than these as well.

The fourth reason: that the scholar stipulates some conditions for the acceptance of *ḥadīth* which was transmitted by one trustworthy memorizer but is opposed by others [who do not accept such conditions]. For instance, some stipulate that the *ḥadīth* must be compared to what is in the Qur'ān and the established *Sunnah*;[84] or that the transmitter must be a jurist if his narration happens to oppose that which can be deduced from textual principles (*qiyās al-uṣūl*);[85] or the stipulation by some that the narration of the *ḥadīth* needs to be widespread and known if it deals with an issue known to have occurred frequently at the time of the Prophet.[86] There are other conditions, well-known within their respective places [of discussion].

The fifth reason: that the *ḥadīth* has reached the scholar and its authenticity has been established to him, but he forgets the narration. This can occur with regard to the Qur'ān and the *Sunnah*. For instance, there is the well-known *ḥadīth* related on the authority of 'Umar (may Allah be pleased with him) that he was asked about the person who is in a state of major ritual impurity but finds no water while he is traveling. 'Umar said he must not pray until he finds water. 'Ammār b. Yāsir (may Allah be pleased with him) then said, "O Commander of the Faithful! Do you not remember when you and I were [herding] camels and we were both in states of major ritual impurity and I rolled in the dust and performed prayer while you did not perform your prayer? And [do you not remember] that I mentioned this to the Prophet (peace be on him) and he replied, "It was enough for you to do it in this way" and then he struck the ground with his hands and then wiped his face and hands with his palms?" 'Umar then said: "O 'Ammār, fear Allah!" So 'Ammār said, "If you so wish, I will not narrate it," upon which 'Umar remarked, "We hold you responsible for what you claim."[87]

Thus, this is a *sunnah* which was witnessed by 'Umar (may Allah be pleased with him) and one which he later forgot. Moreover, he even issued a *fatwā* opposing it and even when 'Ammār (may Allah be pleased with him) sought to remind him he failed to remember. Despite this, he did not accuse 'Ammār of lying but instead [implicitly] ordered him to narrate this *ḥadīth*.

---

[84] See, Aḥmad b. al-Ḥusayn al-Bayhaqī, *al-Qirā'ah Khalf al-Imām* (Beirut: Dār al-Kutub al-'Ilmiyyah, 1405 AH), 203; 'Umar b. 'Alī Ibn al-Mulaqqin, *Tadhkirat al-Muḥtāj ilā Aḥādīth al-Minhāj* (Beirut: al-Maktab al-Islāmī, 1994), 27 and 'Abd al-Raḥmān ibn Abī Bakr al-Suyūtī, *Miftāḥ al-Jannah fī 'l-Iḥtijāj bi 'l-Sunnah* (al-Madīnah al-Munawwarah: Madīnah University, 1399 AH), 10.

[85] See, Ibn Rushd, *Bidāyat al-Mujtahid*, 2: 216; al-Shawkānī, *Nayl*, 5: 332.

[86] See, for instance, 'Alī b. Muḥammad al-Āmidī, *al-Iḥkām fī Uṣūl al-Fiqh* (Beirut: Dār al-Kitāb al-'Arabī, 1404 AH), 2: 124; 'Alī b. Aḥmad Ibn Ḥazm, *al-Iḥkām fī Uṣūl al-Aḥkām* (Cairo: Dār al-Ḥadīth, 1404 AH), 2: 151; Idem, *al-Muḥallā* (Beirut: Dār al-Āfāq al-Jadīdah, n.d.), 4: 117, Yaḥya b. Sharaf al-Nawāwī, *al-Majmū': Sharḥ al-Muhadhdhab* (Beirut: Dār al-Fikr, 1997), 5: 221.

[87] See, Muslim, *Ṣaḥīḥ*, Kitāb al-Ḥayḍ, Bāb al-Tayammum.

More illustrative of this point is [the occasion] when 'Umar delivered a speech to the people in which he stated, "No one must exceed the dowry paid by the Prophet (peace be on him) to his wives and the dowry of his daughters [and if he does] I will return it [to the payer]." A woman then said to him: "O Commander of the Faithful! Why do you deny us what was given to us by Allah?" Then she recited ❨*... and you have given one of them a heap of gold, then take not from it anything*❩.[88] Following this 'Umar retracted his opinion and accepted hers for he had memorised the verse but had forgotten [its relevance].[89]

This is similar to what was narrated about 'Alī who reminded al-Zubayr during the battle of al-Jamal about something which the Prophet (peace be on him) had entrusted to them; so al-Zubayr remembered and gave up the fighting because of it.[90]

Incidences of this kind [i.e. of learning a text and then forgetting it] are frequent among both the early and later scholars.

The sixth reason: that the scholar does not know the implication of the *concerned ḥadīth*. This can be due to the fact that a term mentioned in the *ḥadīth* was considered by him to be unfamiliar (*gharīb*), such as [the terms]: *al-muzābanah, al-mukhābarah, al-muḥāqalah, al-mulāmasah, al-munābadhah, al-gharar* and other such unfamiliar terms about the interpretation of which scholars might disagree. An example is the *ḥadīth* transmitted by a chain attributed back to the Prophet (peace be on him): "No divorce and manumission [of a slave] in a state of *ighlāq*."[91] *Ighlāq* was interpreted [by some] to mean 'coercion' while those who disagreed were not [fully] aware of this [linguistic] interpretation.

It may sometimes also be because the meaning [of the *ḥadīth*] in the scholar's dialect and customary usage which was not [in conformity with] that language employed by the Prophet (peace be on him), so the scholar would

---

[88] Qur'ān 4: 20.

[89] See, 'Abd al-Razzāq, *Muṣannaf*, 6: 180; Sa'īd ibn Manṣūr, *Sunan Sa'īd ibn Manṣūr* (India: al-Dār al-Salafiyyah, 1982), 1: 195. It is also quoted by Muḥammad b. Futūḥ al-Ḥumaydī, *al-Jam' bayn al-Ṣaḥīḥayn: al-Bukhārī wa Muslim* (Beirut: Dār Ibn Ḥazm, 2002), 4: 324. See also, 'Alī b. 'Umar al-Dāraquṭnī, *al-'Ilal al-Wāridah fī 'l-Aḥādīth al-Nabawiyyah* (Riyadh: Dār Ṭaybah, 1985), 2: 232; 'Abd Allāh b. Yūsuf al-Zayla'ī, *Takhrīj al-Aḥādīth wa 'l-Āthār al-Wāqi'ah fī Tafsīr al-Kashshāf li 'l-Zamakhsharī* (Riyadh: Dār Ibn Khuzaymah, 1414 AH), 1: 294–297.

[90] See, Muḥammad b. 'Abd Allāh al-Ḥākim, *al-Mustadrak 'alā al-Ṣaḥīḥayn* (Beirut: Dār al-Kutub al-'Ilmiyyah, 1990), 3: 412–414. See also, Ma'mar b. Rāshid al-Azdī, *al-Jāmi'* published with *al-Muṣannaf* of 'Abd al-Razzāq (Beirut: al-Maktab al-Islāmī, 1403 AH), 11: 241.

[91] See, Ibn Mājah, *Sunan*, Kitāb al-Ṭalāq, Bāb Ṭalāq al-Mukrahi wa al-Nāsī; Aḥmad, *Musnad*, 6: 276; 'Abd Allāh b. Muḥammad Ibn Abī Shaybah, *al-Kitāb al-Muṣannaf fī 'l-Aḥādīth wa 'l-Āthār* (Riyadh: Maktabat al-Rushd, 1409 AH), 4: 83; 'Alī b. 'Umar al-Dāraquṭnī, *Sunan al-Dāraquṭnī* (Beirut: Dār al-Ma'rifah, 1966), 4: 36.

correlate it to what he understood from the term in accordance with his tongue, basing this on the principle that a word retains its original meaning [until proven otherwise].

This is like some of the scholars who heard some reports (*āthār*) which allow a concession with regard to *nabīdh*, so they thought it referred to some types of intoxicants; due to the fact that this term (i.e. *nabīdh*) was used for those [intoxicants] in their native tongue, whereas in reality this term refers to that which was left in the water to sweeten it and was consumed before it attained any intoxicating qualities. This meaning is made clear through several authentic *ḥadīths*.[92]

Similarly, some scholars encountered the term '*khamr*' in the Qur'ān and *Sunnah* and they thought it referred to intoxicants made from grapes only on the basis that this was the meaning of the term in their dialect, but there are authentic *ḥadīth*s which confirm that the term *khamr* is a name for every intoxicating drink.[93]

Sometimes the scholar did not know the implication of the *ḥadīth* because the term [used in that text] was either a homonym, ambivalent in its meaning, or one that hovered between the literal and metaphorical sense, so the scholar took what he thought is the nearest [to the intended meaning] even though the intended meaning may turn out to be the other meaning of the term.

Again, some of the Companions understood the "white thread and the black thread" [in the verse dealing with the time for beginning the fast][94] to refer to an actual rope (*ḥabl*).[95] Others also understood 'hands' in the verse [dealing with dry ablution] ❮*and rub therewith your faces and hands*❯[96] to cover the entire arm up to the armpit.[97]

[The scholar] sometimes [did not know the implication of the *ḥadīth*] because its import was obscure (*khafī*). This is due to the fact that the indications that can be drawn from a statement are often very diverse and so people naturally differ in their ability to comprehend them and to grasp their meaning depending on what Allah has bestowed upon them.

Then a person might know the general implication of a text but he might not recognise that this specific case is included within that general context. It is

---

[92] See, for instance, Muslim, *Ṣaḥīḥ*, Kitāb al-Ḥajj, Bāb Wujūb al-Mabīt bi Minā; Abū Dāwūd, *Sunan*, Kitāb al-Ashribah, Bāb Ṣifat al-Nabīdh.

[93] See, Muslim, *Ṣaḥīḥ*, Kitāb al-Ashribah, Bāb Bayān anna Kull Muskir Khamr.

[94] Qur'ān 2: 186.

[95] This verse was revealed in the context of setting the time for beginning the fasting which is at dawn time.

[96] Qur'ān 4: 43.

[97] This verse was revealed in the context of dry ablution (*al-tayammum*).

possible that he might recognise that this specific case is included under that general context but then he forgets this later on. This is such a vast subject that can be encompassed by none but Allah. It is also possible that a person commits a mistake by deriving from a statement what is not conceivable within the Arabic language which the Prophet (peace be on him) was sent with.

The seventh reason: that the scholar thought that the *hadīth* did not carry any specific implication (*dalālah*).

The difference between this reason and the one before it is that in the previous [instance] the scholar did not know that specific implication whereas in this reason he knows the specific implication but believes that it ought not to be applied based on some principles he had which invalidated that implication, regardless of whether he was in reality right or wrong.

Examples of those principles include: that the scholar believes the specified general text (*al-ʿāmm al-makhṣūṣ*) is not a valid proof, or that the implication (*al-mafhūm*) is not a valid proof,[98] or that a general ruling established for a specific cause is applied only where that cause exists, or that a general imperative does not necessitate obligation or immediate compliance, or that the *alif* and *lām* [constituents of the Arabic definite article] do not denote generality, or that negated verbs neither negate its essence nor all of its rulings, or that the required meaning (*al-muqtaḍā*) does not necessitate a general import and as a result he would not claim the existence of a general import in the omitted elements (*al-muḍmarāt*) and the effective cause [*al-maʿānī*].[99]

And likewise with other examples which would need a lengthy discussion were we to delve into them, as indeed half of the disputes that have arisen in *uṣūl al-fiqh* come within this field [i.e. the implications]; even though the absolute principles [i.e. Qurʾān and *Ḥadīth*] do not encompass all of the disputed implications. One of the questions in this topic is whether certain sub-categories of classes of implications are included under the main class or not. For instance, a scholar might believe that a certain term is ambivalent (*mujmal*) due to the fact that it is a homonym (*mushtarak*), and there is nothing to indicate the preference of one of its two meanings over the other, or other [such] examples.

---

[98] For details related to the discussion on the authority of the implications, see, ʿAbd al-Malik b. ʿAbd Allāh al-Juwaynī, *al-Burhān fī Uṣūl al-Fiqh* (Cairo: al-Wafāʾ, 1418 AH), 1: 298; Idem, *al-Talkhīṣ fī Uṣūl al-Fiqh* (Beirut: Dār al-Bashāʾir al-Islāmiyyah, 1996), 2: 184; ʿAbd Allāh b. Aḥmad Ibn Qudāmah, *Rawḍat al-Nāḍir wa Junnat al-Munāẓir* (Riyadh: The Imām University, 1399), 262; al-Āmidī, *al-Iḥkām*, 3: 73.

[99] See, Āl Taymiyyah: ʿAbd al-Salām b. ʿAbd Allāh, ʿAbd al-Ḥalīm b. ʿAbd al-Salām and Aḥmad b. ʿAbd al-Ḥalīm, *al-Musawwadah fī uṣūl al-Fiqh*, ed. Muḥammad Muḥyī ʾl-Dīn ʿAbd al-Ḥamīd (Cairo: Maṭbaʿ al-Madanī, 1964), 81.

The eighth reason: that the scholar deems that implication of the text to be opposed by something indicating that it could not have been so intended. Examples include a general term being opposed by a specific one, an absolute term (*al-muṭlaq*) by a qualified one (*al-muqayyad*), an absolute imperative by that which negates it, or the literal (*al-ḥaqīqah*) one by that which indicates a metaphor (*al-majāz*), and so on. This is also a vast subject; for indeed the conflict between the numerous implications of a phrase and the task of giving preference to some of them over others is like a wide ocean.

The ninth reason: that the scholar thinks that the *ḥadīth* is opposed by contrary evidence which is accepted by all scholars, such as a Qur'ānic verse, another *ḥadīth*, or consensus, thereby indicating the *ḥadīth*'s weakness, abrogation, or interpretation, if it is amenable to interpretation. This is of two types:

First: that the scholar believes that the contrary evidence is preferable (*rājiḥ*) in general, leading to one of the three possibilities [that is, the weakening of the *ḥadīth*, its abrogation, or its interpretation away from the undesirable meaning] without specifying any one of them.

Second: that the scholar specifies one of the three, so he believes that the proof is abrogated or interpreted away. There is the possibility, however, that he might commit a mistake regarding the abrogation by considering the later evidence to be the earlier one. Alternatively, he might err in interpretation by understanding the *ḥadīth* in a way which its wording does not permit, or where there is something extraneous which rules out that interpretation.

And if the new evidence was to oppose the earlier evidence in general terms, there might be a possibility that the opposing evidence does not give rise to the meaning which the scholar understood. It is also possible that the opposing *ḥadīth* is not equal in strength to the first one in terms of the authenticity of its chain of transmitters and the clarity of its text (*matn*). The same points and others apart from them could of course also be said for the first *ḥadīth*.

In most cases the claim of a consensus is actually no more than the absence of knowledge about any opposing opinion. And we have found among the distinguished scholars those who arrived at certain opinions on the basis of the non-existence of any contrary opinion, even though the apparent meaning of the evidence necessitates, according to them, other than that opinion. It was unthinkable, however, for that scholar to espouse an opinion which was not known to have been held by any earlier scholar, despite knowing that the people disagree with that view, to the extent that some scholars qualify their opinion by saying, "If there is a consensus on this issue then it is the most deserving to be followed. If not, I think the ruling with regard to this issue is such and such."[100]

An example of this is the statement of the one who says, "I do not know anyone who allowed the testimony of a slave" whereas the acceptance of it is narrated from 'Alī, Anas, Shurayḥ, and others.[101] Another is the saying, "It is agreed that the partially freed slave does not inherit" whereas this right of inheritance is narrated from 'Alī and Ibn Mas'ūd (may Allah be pleased with them) and there is a *ḥasan ḥadīth* from the Prophet (peace be on him) to that effect.[102] And finally, "I do not know of anyone who made obligatory the prayer upon the Prophet (peace be on him) in the prayer" whereas its obligation is narrated from Abū Ja'far al-Bāqir.[103]

This is due to the fact that the ultimate aim for many scholars is to know the opinions of the scholars who were their contemporaries within their region while not knowing the opinions of other scholars. We also find many of the early scholars who only knew the opinions of the Madīnans and Kūfans, and many later scholars only knew two or three opinions from amongst those of the reputed scholars, while anything outside this was considered by them to be opposed to the consensus because they did not know of any statement to the contrary [from a reputed scholar] even though they always heard views opposing what they knew.

It will not be possible for such a person to use a *ḥadīth* opposed to this alleged consensus, because of his fear that this will lead to opposing consensus or that he believes that it does actually oppose the consensus, whilst [in his mind] consensus is the greatest of evidences. This is the extenuating reason of many people in many cases where they did not adhere to the obvious import of the evidence. Some of them in reality can be excused, whereas others cannot be excused. This is also true with regard to the aforementioned and later reasons.

The tenth reason: [the scholar thought that] the *ḥadīth* was opposed by evidence indicating the *ḥadīth*'s weakness, abrogation, or contrary interpretation, whereas his view that this is a contrary evidence is not shared by other scholars, or even by those who belong to his group, or the contrary evidence is not in reality the prevalent one.

---

[100] See, Muḥammad ibn Mufliḥ al-Maqdisī, *al-Furū' fī 'l-Fiqh al-Ḥanblī* (Beirut: Dār al-Kutub al-'Ilmiyyah, 1418 AH), 5: 447 and Muḥammad ibn Abī Bakr b. Ayyūb known as Ibn al-Qayyim, *Aḥkām Ahl al-Dhimmah* (Dammam- Beirut: Ramadī, 1997), 2: 747, 793.

[101] See for example, al-Bukhārī, *Ṣaḥīḥ*, Kitāb al-Shahādāt, Bāb Shahādat al-Imā' wa 'l-'Abīd.

[102] See, Aḥmad b. Shu'ayb al-Nasā'ī, *al-Sunan al-Kubrā*, Kitāb al-Qisāmah, Bab Diyat al-Mukātab.

[103] See, al-Ṭabarī, *Tahdhīb al-Āthār*, 257; Ismā'īl b. 'Umar Ibn Kathīr, *Tafsīr al-Qur'ān al-'Aẓīm* (Beirut: Dār al-Fikr, 1401 AH), 3: 509; al-Shawkānī, *Nayl al-Awṭār*, 2: 321–326; al-Zayla'ī, *Naṣb al-Rāyah*, 1: 427.

An example of this is of the approach of many of the Kūfans who, when an authentic *ḥadīth* is opposed by the apparent meaning of a Qur'ānic text, believe that the apparent Qur'ānic text, such as one expressing generality, is given preference over the explicit meaning of a *ḥadīth*.

A scholar might consider something to be apparent which is not in reality apparent; this is because there are many potential implications of a statement. So, as a result, the *ḥadīth* of "the witness and the oath"[104] was rejected by the Kūfans [on the basis that it was in opposition to an apparent Qur'ānic text], even though other scholars know that there is nothing in the apparent Qur'ānic text to prevent giving judgement in favour of someone on the basis of one witness and the claimant's oath. And if it should be the case [i.e. even if an apparent Qur'ānic text opposing this *ḥadīth* was to be found], then, according to these scholars the *Sunnah* is the 'interpreter' of the Qur'ān. And there are well known statements from al-Shāfiʿī regarding this principle. Also, Aḥmad [ibn Ḥanbal] has his well known book on the refutation of the opinion of those who claimed the sufficiency of apparent Qur'ānic texts (*ẓāhir al-Qur'ān*) without the need to interpret such texts with the *Sunnah* of the Prophet (peace be on him). He mentioned in it evidences which the limitation of space prevents us from mentioning here.

And another example of this is to reject the *ḥadīth* (*al-khabar*) which specifies the general meaning of a Qur'ānic text, or which qualifies an absolute Qur'ānic text, or adds to the Qur'ānic ruling. The belief of those who say this is that adding to a text, as well as qualifying an absolute text, is a form of abrogation, and specifying a general text is also [a form of] abrogation.

Another example concerns a group of the Madīnans who oppose authentic *ḥadīth*s in preference to the practice of the people of Madīnah, on the basis that they (i.e. *ahl al-Madīnah*) must have been in agreement not to act upon those *ḥadīth*s, and their agreement is a proof which is given preference over the *ḥadīth*. For instance, they did not act upon the *ḥadīth*s related to the right of withdrawal from transactions (*khiyār al-majlis*)[105] on the basis of this principle. Most scholars, however, affirm the existence of disagreement among the Madīnans on this issue [that is, regarding the right of withdrawal from transactions] but state that even if the Madīnans were in agreement and they were opposed by other scholars [who are supported by *Ḥadīth* evidences], then the most authoritative source would be the *Ḥadīth*.

---

[104] See, Mālik, *Muwaṭṭa'*, 2: 721; Aḥmad, *Musnad*, 3: 305; Abū Dāwūd, *Sunan*, Kitāb al-Aqdiyah, Bāb al-Qaḍā' bi 'l-Yamīn wa 'l-Shāhid; al-Tirmidhī, *Sunan*, Kitāb al-Aḥkām, Bāb mā jā' fī 'l-Yamīn maʿ al-Shāhid; al-Nasā'ī, *al-Sunan al-Kubrā*, Kitāb al-Qaḍā', Bāb al-Ḥukm bi al-Yamīn wa 'l-Shāhid.

[105] See, Muslim, *Ṣaḥīḥ*, Kitāb al-Buyūʿ, Bāb Thubūt Khiyār al-Majlis.

Another example is that of some people of the two cities (Madīnah and Kūfah) opposing some *ḥadīths* with explicit analogy (*qiyās jalī*) arguing that general principles cannot be refuted by such *ḥadīths*.

And so on with similar areas of dispute regardless of whether the scholar opposing the *ḥadīth* is right or wrong. So, these ten reasons are clear.

It is possible in many cases that the scholar has a proof for not acting upon a *ḥadīth* which we are not aware of because the ways of comprehending knowledge are manifold and we cannot know all of what is in the hearts of the scholars. The scholar might have mentioned his proof or might not have, and if he were to mention it, it may or may not have reached us; and even if it was to reach us we may or may not comprehend the thrust of his argument, irrespective of whether his proof was in reality correct or not.

However, if we allow this possibility [that the proof supporting a *mujtahid*'s argument is unknown to us], it is not permitted for us to turn away from an opinion whose authority is established by an authentic *ḥadīth* and is followed by some people of knowledge for another opinion proclaimed by another scholar who might possibly have an answer to that proof, even if he was more knowledgeable [than the first scholar]. This is due to the fact that the opinions of scholars are more prone to error then the *sharʿī* evidence itself. The *sharʿī* evidences are Allah's proof against all of his servants and this is not the case with regard to the opinion of the scholar. Indeed, it is impossible for the *sharʿī* evidences to contain error if they are not contradicted by other similar evidence and this cannot be said for the opinion of a scholar.

And if practicing this [i.e. following the opinion of a scholar in the face of an opposing *sharʿī* evidence] were to be allowed, then none of the evidences which accept this possibility [i.e. being open to *ijtihād*] will remain as such.

However, the purpose [of what we mentioned earlier] is that the scholar might have had a valid excuse for not following the *sharʿī* evidence, and we are excused for not following his opinion. And Allah (Glorified and Exalted is He!) says: ❴*This is a people that have passed away; they shall have what they earned and you shall have what you earn, and you shall not be called upon to answer for what they did.*❵[106]

And Allah (Glorified is He!) also said, (*And if you have a dispute concerning any matter, refer it to Allah and the Messenger if you are (in truth) believers in Allah and the Last Day.*)[107]

It is not permitted for anyone to oppose an authentic *ḥadīth* of the Prophet (peace be on him) and give preference to the opinion of any human being. On one occasion, when Ibn ʿAbbās (may Allah be pleased with him and

---

[106] Qurʾān 2: 134.

[107] Qurʾān 4: 59.

his father) was asked by a man about an issue, he answered with a *ḥadīth*. The man responded, "[But] Abū Bakr and 'Umar said such and such [with regard to that issue]," Ibn 'Abbās said: "You are about to be struck by stones from the sky! I say to you that the Prophet (peace be on him) said such and such, and you reply, "[But] Abū Bakr and 'Umar said such and such!""[108]

If it is accepted that some of the reasons mentioned above could cause a scholar to not follow a *sharʿī* evidence, and if an authentic *ḥadīth* is found which contains permissibility, prohibition or another ruling, it is not permissible to believe that a scholar who did not adhere to it (whose reasons for departing from the text have been given above) should be punished because he made the prohibited permissible or vice versa, or that he gave judgement on the basis of what was not revealed by Allah. Similarly, if a *ḥadīth* contains a threat, by the mention of a *la'n*,[109] anger or punishment, or something similar, then it is not permitted to say that the scholar, who permitted such an action or undertook it, would fall within the purview of that threat. We know of no disagreement among the scholars of the *ummah* with regard to this issue except something narrated from some of the Baghdādī Mu'tazilites such as Bishr al-Marrīsī[110] and his like who alleged that those among the *mujtahids* who make a mistake would be punished on account of this mistake. This is because the one who commits a prohibited action would be liable for the threat only if he was aware of the prohibition or if he was able to obtain that knowledge and failed to do so. As for those who are brought up in the *bādiyah* [remote places away from civilisation], or are new converts to Islam and who commit a prohibited action without being aware of its prohibition, they will not be sinning, and they cannot be punished with prescribed punishments (*ḥudūd*) even if they did not base their action on *sharʿī* evidence. Therefore, *a fortiori*, those who were not aware of the prohibiting *ḥadīth* and based the permissibility of an action upon *sharʿī* evidence are more deserving to be

---

[108] See, Muḥammad al-Amīn b. Muḥammad al-Mukhtār al-Shanqīṭī, *Aḍwā' al-Bayān* (Beirut: Dār al-Fikr li 'l-Ṭibā'ah wa 'l-Nashr, 1995), 7: 328.

[109] What is meant by *la'n* here, according to the classical Muslim literature, is to pray or state that a person be rejected from the mercy of God permanently or temporarily. But it could also mean in some instances censure and condemnation of the action with which the *la'n* was associated. See, Muḥammad b. Jarīr al-Ṭabarī, *Jāmi' al-Bayān 'an Ta'wīl Āyy al-Qur'ān* (Beirut: Dār al-Fikr, 1405 AH), 1: 408; Ibn Qudāmah, *al-Mughnī*, 8: 39; al-Nawāwī, *Ṣaḥīḥ Muslim bi Sharḥ al-Nawāwī*, 9: 140–141; Muḥammad b. Makram Ibn Manẓūr, *Lisān al-'Arab* (Beirut: Dār Ṣādir, n.d.), 13: 387; Muḥammad ibn Abī Bakr al-Rāzī, *Mukhtār al-Ṣiḥāḥ* (Beirut: Maktabat Lebanon, 1995), 250.

[110] See, Aḥmad b. 'Alī al-Khaṭīb al-Baghdādī, *Ta'rīkh Baghdād* (Beirut: Dār al-Kutub al-'Ilmiyyah, n.d.) 7: 56–66; Aḥmad b. 'Alī Ibn Ḥajar, *Lisān al-Mīzān* (Beirut: Mu'assasat al-A'lāmī, 1986), 2: 29.

excused. This is why such a scholar is rewarded and praised because of his independent reasoning. Allah (the Exalted) says: ❨*And remember David and Solomon, when they gave judgement in the matter of the field into which the sheep of certain people had strayed by night: We did witness their judgement. To Solomon We inspired the (right) understanding of the matter: to each (of them) We gave Judgement and Knowledge*❩.[111]

So Solomon was distinguished for his understanding [in this case] while both were praised for [having] sound judgement and knowledge. In the two *Ṣaḥīḥ*s of al-Bukhārī and Muslim it is narrated on the authority of 'Amr b. al-'Āṣ (may Allah be pleased with him) that the Prophet (peace be on him) said, "When a judge exercises independent reasoning and gives the right judgement, he will have two rewards, but if he errs in his judgement, he will still have earned one reward."[112]

Therefore, it is clear that the *mujtahid*, despite his error, is rewarded because of his *ijtihād* and his mistake is forgiven due to the fact that arriving at the correct opinion on every occasion is either impossible or highly unlikely. And Allah the Exalted says, ❨*And Allah has not laid upon you in religion any hardship*❩[113] and He said, ❨*Allah desires ease for you, and He does not desire for you difficulty*❩.[114]

In the two *Ṣaḥīḥ*s of al-Bukhārī and Muslim it is narrated that the Prophet (peace be on him) said to his Companions in the Year of the Trench, "None of you should pray the *'Aṣr* prayer until you reach Banū Qurayẓah" and so when it was time for *'Aṣr* prayer and the companions were still on their way, some of them said. "We will not pray (*'Aṣr* prayer) until we arrive at Banū Qurayẓah [i.e. even if the time for *'Aṣr* prayer elapses]." Others said that this was not the intended meaning and they prayed *'Aṣr* prayer while on the way and the Prophet found no fault with either of the two groups.[115]

The first group held to the generality of the communication (*'umūm al-khiṭāb*) and therefore they considered the lapse of the appointed time [for the Prayer] as being included under that generality. The other group felt they had the evidence necessitating the exclusion of this [the lapse of the appointed time] from the general import of the communication. They understood the command to be an encouragement to them to make haste in reaching those

---

[111] Qur'ān 21: 78–79.

[112] Al-Bukhārī, *Ṣaḥīḥ*, Kitāb al-I'tiṣām, Bāb Ajr al-Ḥākim idhā Ijtahada; Muslim, *Ṣaḥīḥ*, Kitāb al-Aqḍiyah, Bāb Bayān Ajr al-Ḥākim idhā Ijtahad.

[113] Qur'ān 22: 78.

[114] Qur'ān 2: 185.

[115] See, al-Bukhārī, *Ṣaḥīḥ*, Kitāb al-Jumu'ah, Bāb Ṣalāt al-Ṭālib wa 'l-Maṭlūb Rākiban wa Īmā'an; Muslim, *Ṣaḥīḥ*, Kitāb al-Jihād, Bāb al-Mubādarah bi 'l-Ghazw.

that the Prophet (peace be on him) had taken under siege.

This is an issue upon which there is a well known disagreement among the jurists, namely, "Can the general be particularised by analogy?" (*hal yukhaṣṣ al-ʿumūm bi 'l-qiyās*). However, [my view is that] those who prayed on the way were more correct in what they did.

Similarly, when Bilāl (may Allah be pleased with him) sold two *ṣāʿ* of one type of dates for one *ṣāʿ* of another type of dates, the Prophet (peace be on him) ordered him to return it[116] [on the basis that this was a transaction involving *ribā*] but he did not indicate that Bilāl came within the sphere of the rulings for consuming *ribā* such as depravity (*tafsīq*), condemnation (*al-laʿn*) and sternness (*taghlīẓ*); because Bilāl had not been aware that this transaction was prohibited.

Also, ʿAdī b. Ḥātim and a group of the Companions (may Allah be pleased with them) thought that the Qurʾānic verse ❨...*until you can identify the white thread from the black thread*❩[117] referred to [the literal meaning of the word *al-khayṭ*] i.e. the white rope and the black rope. So one of them would leave two strings near his pillow, one white and the other black, and would eat until he could identify one from the other. Upon learning of this, the Prophet (peace be on him) said to ʿAdī, "Your pillow seems to be very large! It is only the whiteness of the dawn and the blackness of the night."[118]

Therefore, the Prophet (peace be on him) indicated by this that ʿAdī had not correctly comprehended the meaning of the verse, yet the Prophet did not attribute to him the censure of one who did not observe the fasting of Ramaḍān, even though it is one of the major sins.

In contrast [to this] are those who gave a *fatwā* to a man who had a head-injury (in the skull) that he had to wash the whole of his body [i.e. due to being in a state of major ritual impurity] so he did. He died as a result and the Prophet (peace be on him) said, "They killed him; may Allah kill them! Should not they have asked if they did not know? Indeed, the cure for ignorance is inquiry."[119]

Hence these people committed a mistake without [proper] *ijtihād* as they were not from among the people of knowledge.

---

[116] See, al-Bukhārī, *Ṣaḥīḥ*, Kitāb al-Wakālah, Bāb idhā Bāʿ al-Wakīl Shayʾan Fāsid; Muslim, *Ṣaḥīḥ*, Kitāb al-Musāqāh, Bāb Bayʿ al-Ṭaʿām Mithlan bi Mithl.

[117] Qurʾān 2: 187.

[118] See, al-Bukhārī, *Ṣaḥīḥ*, Kitāb al-Tafsīr, Bāb wa Kulū waʾshrabū; Muslim, *Ṣaḥīḥ*, Kitāb al-Ṣiyām, Bāb Bayān ann al-Dukhūl fī 'l-Ṣawm Yaḥṣulu bi Ṭulūʿ al-Fajr.

[119] See, ʿAbd al-Razzāq, *Muṣannaf*, 1: 223; Aḥmad, *Musnad*, 1: 330; Abū Dāwūd, *Sunan*, Kitāb al-Ṭahārah, Bāb fī 'l-Majrūḥ Yatayammam; Ibn Mājah, *Sunan*, Kitāb al-Ṭahārah, Bāb fī 'l-Majrūḥ Tuṣībuh al-Janābah.

Another example is that the Prophet (peace be on him) did not impose retaliation, blood money or expiation upon Usāmah b. Zayd when he killed the person who had testified that "There is no God but Allah" in the battle of al-Ḥuraqāt.[120] Usāmah believed that it was permissible to kill him on the basis that his Islam was invalid, even though it is clear that his killing was unlawful. The *salaf* and the majority of the jurists acted upon this when they concluded that the rebels would not be liable for retaliation, blood-money or expiation, in cases such as shedding the blood of innocent people, which they legitimated on grounds of some plausible reason (*ta'wīl sā'igh*), they [rebels] will not be held responsible even though the killing and fighting they engaged in were prohibited.[121]

The aforementioned condition for the applicability of a threat does not need to be repeated in every communication because the knowledge of it is well known and established in the hearts.

This is just like the promise [of reward] for carrying out a good deed is prefaced upon its being done with sincerity for the sake of Allah and that the deed was not rendered void by apostasy. This condition, also, is not mentioned in every *hadīth* which promises a reward for an action.

And even when the conditions necessitating the applicability of a threat are present, the threat might be removed through the existence of an impediment (*māni'*). There are various types of such impediments, including repentance, asking for forgiveness, good deeds that erase sins, tribulations and calamities, the intercession of someone whose intercession is accepted and the mercy of the Most Merciful.

It is only when all of these impediments are lacking—and this will not be the case except with regard to the one who was arrogant, rebellious and fled from Allah in a way similar to that of a camel straying from its people—that the threat will be duly applicable to him. This is because the main function of a threat is to emphasise that the deed in question is a cause for the punishment mentioned in the threat, thus creating the inference that the deed is prohibited and reprehensible. However, to say that the existence of the reason for the threat in any person would necessitate the occurrence of the consequence (i.e the punishment) is indeed an absolutely invalid conclusion. [As we have explained], the effect of a threat depends upon the presence of its conditions and the removal of all of the impediments to it.

---

[120] See, al-Bukhārī, *Ṣaḥīḥ*, Kitāb al-Diyāt, Bāb Qawl Allāh Ta'ālā wa man Aḥyāhā; Muslim, *Ṣaḥīḥ*, Kitāb al-Īmān, Bāb Taḥrīm Qatl al-Kāfir ba'd an Qāl Lā Ilāh illā 'llāh.

[121] What Ibn Taymiyyah is discussing here is the issue of giving amnesty to rebels and, as he asserts somewhere else, non-belief is not a legitimate reason for killing.

To clarify this further, there are three possibilities with regard to the one who did not act upon a given *ḥadīth*:

First: that his leaving the *ḥadīth* is permissible according to the agreement of all Muslims. An example of this is the person who did not act upon a *ḥadīth* because he was not aware of it, although he had sought to the best of his ability to find out about it in view of his need for a *fatwā* or a judicial ruling, as we mentioned in the case of the rightly guided Caliphs and others (may Allah be pleased with them). There is no doubt in any Muslim's mind that such a person will not be liable for the sin resulting from the neglect of a deed [due to ignorance of the existence of the obligation/prohibition].

Second: that the leaving of the *ḥadīth* is not permissible. It is highly unlikely that we will find the Imāms not acting upon a *ḥadīth* without a legitimate reason, God (the Exalted) willing.

[Third:] What might be possible, however, is that some scholars may sometimes give an opinion on an issue despite the fact that they did not fully comprehend the issue in question, so they would give their opinion without having fulfilled the proper requirements for giving a ruling on that issue, even though they have some understanding and capacity for *ijtihād* on it.

[It is also possible that] the scholar is deficient in his deduction, so he would conclude with an opinion without an evidence for such conclusion even though he might have used some form of *ijtihād* or he would arrive at his opinion before having taken his reasoning to its appropriate conclusion, even where he is basing his opinion on some evidence, or he might be influenced by a custom or predisposition which prevents him from an exhaustive treatment of the issue which would include a study of that which opposes his view, even if he based his opinion on some *ijtihād* and reasoning. This is due to the fact that the [precise] limit [or extent] to which it is necessary to determine *ijtihād* might not be precisely identified by the *mujtahid*.

This is the reason that the scholars used to fear that the recognised form of *ijtihād* (*al-Ijtihād al-Muʿtabar*) might not have been achieved on a given issue. This is indeed a sin but the punishment for the sin is only applicable if its performer did not repent. Moreover, the sin can be erased by asking for forgiveness, doing good to others, [undergoing] tribulation, intercession, and Allah's Mercy.

However, not included under this [i.e. the one who is pardoned] is the one who is overcome and defeated by his desire to the extent that he supports what he knows to be false, or the one who asserts authoritatively the correctness or error of an opinion without knowing the evidence for what he claims, either in affirmation or negation. Indeed, these two are in the Hellfire, as the Prophet (peace be on him) said, "The judges are of three types: two in the Hellfire and one in Paradise; as for the one in Paradise, it is a person who knew the truth so he judged according to it. As for those who are in the Hellfire: it is the one who gave judgement among the people on the basis of ignorance and the one who knew the truth but gave judgement contrary to it."[122]

This is also true with regard to the *muftīs* but there are impediments for the applicability of a threat to a specific person, as we explained earlier.

If the occurrence of something like that was theoretically possible from some of the distinguished scholars who are praised by the *ummah*—even though it is remote (or even non-existent)—he will [surely] not be short of one of the aforementioned reasons [which nullify the threat]. And even if such an occurrence were to be found, this would not diminish their stature as Imāms at all. This is because we do not believe that these people are infallible; rather we accept that they are capable of sin, and at the same time we wish for them the highest of ranks in Paradise because of what they were granted by Allah of righteous deeds and high status, and that they were never persistent in committing sin. We say also that they were not superior in rank to the Companions (may Allah be pleased with them). Furthermore, we say with regard [to the Companions] that which we said regarding the Imāms, in reference to their *ijtihād* in *fatwās*, judgements, and the spilling of blood which occurred between them (may Allah be pleased with them all) and other matters [related to their *ijtihād*].

Having said that [the scholar] who did not act upon a given text is not only excused but even rewarded [i.e. for his *ijtihād*], this does not prevent us from following the authentic *ḥadīths* in respect of which we know of no opposing evidence, neither does it prevent us from believing that it is an obligation upon the *ummah* to act upon them [i.e. authentic *ḥadīths*] and to narrate them—and there is no disagreement among the scholars with regard to this.

Moreover, these *ḥadīths* are of two types:

[The first is the definite *ḥadīth*]; the scholars are in agreement upon the obligation of knowing and acting upon them. This is because both the chains of transmission and the contents (*matan*) of these *ḥadīths* are of definite (*qaṭʿī*) nature. We have certainty that the Messenger of God (peace be on him) uttered such a *ḥadīth* as well as that he intended by it that specific form.

The second is a *ḥadīth* of probable, rather than definite, proof.

As for the first type, it is obligatory to believe in its implication in theory and in practice and there is no disagreement in general among the scholars

---

[122] See, Abū Dāwūd, *Sunan*, Kitāb al-Aqḍiyah, Bāb fī 'l-Qāḍī Yukhṭiʾ; al-Nasāʾī, *al-Sunan al-Kubrā*, Kitāb al-Qaḍāʾ, Bāb Thawāb al-Iṣābah fī 'l-Ḥukm.

with regard to this. They might of course differ with regard to some narrations (*al-akhbār*), as to whether they have definite chains of transmission or not and whether the implication of a narration is definite or not. An example of this is their disagreement over those solitary *ḥadīth*s which were either received by the *ummah* with conviction and belief or which they agreed to act upon. According to the majority of jurists and most Muslim theologians (*mutakallimūn*), this type of *ḥadīth* creates certainty, while some groups of the *mutakallimūn* disagreed.

Similarly, a *ḥadīth* which is transmitted from various channels, each corroborating the other from certain specific authorities, might lead to certain knowledge for the one who is aware of all those channels [of transmission], the status of the transmitters as well as circumstantial and supporting evidences that encompass the narrations; whereas this certainty might be hidden from another scholar who does not possess this information. This is why the leading scholars of *Hadīth* who possessed both a critical mind and an exacting approach to knowledge (may Allah be pleased with them) might reach absolute certainty with regard to some narrations whereas other scholars might not even believe in that authenticity let alone the certainty of such authenticity.

This is based on the fact that the narrations which lead to certainty do so on occasions from the multiplicity of their reporters and at other times from the status of these narrators; through the act of narrating itself; through the perception of the one who receives the narration or from the content of the narration.

So a narration transmitted by a few transmitters might lead to certain knowledge because of that which is known regarding their piety and strong memory, such that it preserved them from being implicated with lying and error. On the other hand, multiple numbers of the same figures from other transmitters might not lead to such certainty. This is no doubt the correct opinion, and it is the opinion of the majority of jurists and *Hadīth* scholars as well as groups from among the *mutakallimūn*.

On the other hand, some groups of the *mutakallimūn* and some jurists adhered to the opinion that if a number of transmitters led to certainty in one case, then this same number of other transmitters must lead to certainty in every case. There can be no doubt that this is utterly incorrect, but this is not the right place to discuss this.

As for the question of the influence of circumstantial evidence that is not related to the transmitters of the *Hadīth*, we have not mentioned it because this circumstantial evidence might lead to certainty by itself. And if it was to lead to certainty by itself then it should not be considered as dependent on the narration without restriction, just as the narration is not dependent on the circumstantial evidence. Rather, both may lead to certainty at one time or probability at another, and sometimes they may come together to create certainty while at other times certainty may arise from one of them and only probability from the other.

A person who has superior knowledge in the field of narrations might be more certain with regard to the authenticity of some narrations, whereas others who are not of his calibre might not attain that level of certainty.

Sometimes the scholars also differ with regard to whether a given *ḥadīth* is definitive or not because of their disagreement over whether the *ḥadīth* is explicit (*naṣṣ*) or apparent (*ẓāhir*) in its implication, and if it is apparent whether it contains something which can exclude the less likely meaning. This too is a vast subject, as some scholars might be convinced of the certainity of implication of some *ḥadīth*s, whereas others do not share that view with them. The first group might be certain that the given *ḥadīth* can only admit that particular meaning, or that it is not allowed to interpret the *ḥadīth* in accordance with the other meaning, or because of some other evidence that leads them to achieve certainty of interpretation.

With regard to the second type, that is the apparent (*al-ẓāhir*) text, all recognised scholars subscribe to the opinion that it is obligatory to act upon it in legal matters. If, on the other hand, it contains a ruling pertaining to belief, such as a threat [of chastisement] and similar notions, the scholars have differed over it:

Some groups from amongst the jurists adhere to the opinion that if a threat of punishment is promised for the commission of an action contained in the narration of a trustworthy solitary transmitter, then it is obligatory to act upon it and to consider that deed as prohibited, but the *ḥadīth* will not actually be used to establish the threat itself unless the narration was definite in import. The same applies if the content of a *ḥadīth* was definite [in terms of its authenticity] but only apparent with regard to its implication. The following statement of ‘Ā’ishah (may Allah be pleased with her) was understood according to this principle. ‘Ā’ishah said to the wife of Abū Isḥāq al-Sabī‘ī, "Tell Zayd b. Arqam that he has invalidated his *jihād* with the Prophet (peace be on him) unless he repents."[123] Thus they argued that ‘Ā’ishah expressed this threat because she was knowledgeable and certain of it. We, however, are obliged to act upon her narration in establishing the prohibition even though we do not hold this threat of punishment due to the fact that the *ḥadīth* has only reached us through a solitary narration. These

---

[123] See for the full text, ‘Abd al-Razzāq, *Muṣannaf*, 8: 185; al-Dāraquṭnī, *Sunan*, 3: 52.

scholars point out that the threat of punishment is a matter of belief and can only be affirmed through a definite (*qaṭ'ī*) text. Moreover, if the ruling on the action is the subject of *ijtihād*, its doer will not be liable to the threat. According to the opinion of this group, the *ḥadīth*s pertaining to threats can be used to establish the prohibition of deeds generally, but the punishment itself is not established unless the meaning of the *ḥadīth* is unequivocal.

Another example is the reliance of most scholars upon the variant readings of the Qur'ān, the authority of which has been established from some of the Companions (may Allah be pleased with them) even though these readings were not in the 'Uthmānic *muṣḥaf* (may Allah be pleased with 'Uthmān). These narrations contained practice and theoretical knowledge and were solitary authentic *ḥadīth*s. They cited these readings to affirm the practice, whilst they did not recognise them as part of the Qur'ān due to the fact that recognising them as part of the Qur'ān is a theoretical issue which cannot be established except through certainty.

Most of the jurists, however, hold the opinion—and this is also the opinion of the generality of the pious predecessors (*salaf*)—that these *ḥadīth*s are authoritative proof in all that they contain of threats because it was the habit of the Companions of the Prophet (peace be on him) and their Successors to affirm threats on the basis of these *ḥadīth*s, just as they also affirmed acting upon them. They would unequivocally declare in general that the threat contained within these *ḥadīth*s is applicable to the one who commits such actions. This is widespread in their narrations and *fatāwā*. Their view is that the threat of punishment falls within those *shar'ī* rulings that can sometimes be established by probable evidence and other times by definite evidence. It is not necessary that there be absolute certainty as regards the threat, but only a belief that is grounded in certainty or a high probability, and this is the case with regard to theoretical rulings.

There is no difference between a person's belief that Allah has prohibited an action and threatened its doer with a general punishment, and his belief that Allah has prohibited an action and threatened its doer with a specific punishment; both of them are ascribed to Allah (the Exalted). Just as it is acceptable to attribute to Him the first category by the use of unrestricted evidence, [i.e. unrestricted in terms of the punishment being unspecified], it is likewise acceptable to attribute to Him through the second type of evidence [which contains a threat of a specific punishment].

Moreover, even if someone were to say that to act upon the threat is more deserving and appropriate, he would be correct. This is why they used to show a degree of leniency in the acceptance of *ḥadīth*s related to moral exhortation (*al-targhīb wa 'l-tarhīb*) that they did not show in the *ḥadīth*s related to legal rulings. [It was felt] that believing in the threat encourages the souls to abstain from prohibited matters. If that threat was true, the person would escape the threatened punishment, and if the threat turned out not to be true, and the consequence of that action would be less severe than that which was threatened, then his mistaken belief that the punishment was greater [than what it was in reality] would not harm him, if he were to leave that action. This is due to the fact that if he had believed that the punishment was less than it was [in reality], he could also have been mistaken. This could also be true if he neither affirmed nor denied the extra punishment, he could still be mistaken.

An erroneous limitation of the punishment might lead him to find it easier to commit the prohibited act and as a result become liable for the extra punishment (if it is established) or it might create a reason for him to deserve such punishment.

Therefore, the possibility of an error in belief using either the existence or non-existence of a punishment is identical; but escaping possible punishment through believing in the existence of a threat is more likely, and so is given preference. It is on the basis of this principle that the majority of scholars give preference to the evidence prohibiting an act over the one permitting the same act.

Many jurists adopted the principle of precaution (al-iḥtiyāṭ) in many rulings on the basis of this argument. Indeed, precaution with regard to action is almost unanimously treated as meritorious among those possessed of wisdom in general.[124]

If an individual's fear of error by denying a threat stands in opposition to his fear of error in the opposite belief, the residual evidence necessitates belief in the existence of the threat and that punishment could be avoided on the basis of that belief [affirming the threat] and these are two evidences free of any opposition.

It is not acceptable for one to say that the non-existence of a definite proof for the threat is an evidence for its non-existence; as it is in the case of the non-existence of *mutawātir* narration for the extra readings not included in the 'Uthmānic *Muṣḥaf*. This is because the non-existence of evidence ('adam al-dalīl) does not necessitate the non-existence of that which is derived (al-madlūl 'alayh).

One who negates one of the theoretical issues on the basis of the absence of definite evidence for its existence—as is the methodology of a group of the scholastic theologians (mutakallimūn)—is in very clear error. However, when

---

[124] For more details on Ibn Taymiyyah and precaution see, Matroudi, *The Hanbali School of Law*, 103–107.

we know that the existence of something necessitates the existence of its proof (*dalīl*), and we are able to affirm non-existence of the proof [whether it be definite or indefinite], then we can assert with certainty the non-existence of that thing. This is on the principle that the absence of the antecedent (*lāzim*) is a proof for the absence of the consequent (*malzūm*).

Having learnt the motivating factors behind the transmission of the Book of Allah and His religion, we know that it is not possible that the *ummah* has concealed that which the people were in need of receiving as a general proof (*ḥujjah ʿāmmah*). Thus, when there is no common narration about a sixth obligatory prayer or another *sūrah* [of the Qurʾān], we know for sure that it does not exist. Having said that, the category of threats does not come under this rule, as it is not a condition for every threatened punishment that it be conveyed in a *mutawātir* manner, just as it is not a condition for establishing the ruling about that action.

It has been established that *ḥadīths* containing threats must be acted upon in accordance with what they indicate, with the conviction that the doer of that action is under the threat associated with the action. Liability for the punishment, however, depends on the existence of certain conditions and there are impediments. This principle can be illustrated with some examples:

It is authentically narrated from the Prophet (peace be on him) that he said: "May Allah reject the receiver of interest, its payer, its witnesses and its scribe."[125] It is also authentically narrated—through more than one authentic chain of transmission—that the Prophet (peace be on him) said to the one who sold two *ṣāʿ*[126] [of one quality] in exchange for one *ṣāʿ* [of another quality]: "Woe to you! This is usury (*ʿayn al-ribā*)."[127] And he also said: "And wheat for wheat amounts to interest unless they are exchanged on the spot ..."[128]

This encapsulates both kinds of interest (*ribā*)—both surplus interest (*ribā 'l-faḍl*)[129] and (*ribā 'l-nasaʾ*),[130] but then those who were aware of the Prophet's statement: "Interest is only in *al-nasīʾah*,"[131] saw it as permissible to exchange two *ṣāʿ* for one *ṣāʿ* in a direct exchange (*yadan bi-yadin*), such as Ibn ʿAbbās (may Allah be pleased with him and his father) and his followers e.g. Abū

---

[125] See, Muslim, *Ṣaḥīḥ*, Kitāb al-Musāqāh, Bāb Laʿn Ākil al-Ribā wa Mukilih.

[126] A measure of volume.

[127] See, n. 116 above.

[128] See, al-Bukhārī, *Ṣaḥīḥ*, Kitāb al-Buyūʿ, Bāb Bayʿ al-Tamr bi al-Tamr; Muslim, *Ṣaḥīḥ*, Kitāb al-Musāqāh, Bāb al-Ṣarf.

[129] Taking something of a superior quality in exchange for more of the same kind of thing but of poorer quality.

[130] Taking interest on loaned money.

[131] See, Muslim, *Ṣaḥīḥ*, Kitāb al-Musāqāh, Bāb Bayʿ al-Ṭaʿām Mithlan bi Mithl.

al-Sha'thā', 'Aṭā', Ṭāwūs, Sa'īd b. Jubayr and 'Ikramah as well as others among the distinguished Makkans who were among the best of this *ummah* in knowledge and practice. It is not permissible for a Muslim to believe that any of them specifically or one who imitates any of them—to the extent that such imitation is permissible—will be liable for the *la'n* mentioned for the one who consumes interest because they did this on the basis of a conceivable interpretation of the texts.

Another example is that which is narrated from a group of the distinguished Madīnans regarding the [matter] of having anal intercourse with the wife despite Abū Dāwūd's narration from the Prophet (peace be on him) that he said, "Whoever has anal intercourse with his wife, he has disbelieved in that which was revealed to Muḥammad."[132] Does anyone think that it is permissible for a Muslim to say that "So and so were disbelievers in that which was revealed to Muḥammad?"

Again, it is established from the Prophet (peace be on him) that he said: "Allah has rejected ten [categories of people] regarding intoxicants (*khamr*): the one who squeezes the juice, the one who asks for it to be squeezed, the one who drinks it ... [etc.]"[133] Moreover, it is also established through various channels that the Prophet (peace be on him) said: "Every intoxicating drink is *khamr*"[134] and he also said: "Every intoxicant is *khamr*."[135] Also, 'Umar (may Allah be pleased with him) said in a speech while on his pulpit in the presence of the Muhājirūn and Anṣār: "*Khamr* is that which befuddles the mind."[136]

Allah revealed the prohibition of *khamr*, and the occasion for its revelation is that they [people] used to drink [it] in Madīnah. They only used to have drinks made from dates, not from grapes at all. Yet there were some among the most eminent Kūfan scholars of this *ummah*—in terms of both practice and knowledge—who believed that *khamr* was derived only from grapes, and that the *nabīdh* produced from other than grapes and the *nabīdh* produced from dates is not prohibited except where the quantity leads to a state of intoxication. They, therefore, drank what they believed to be within the permissible limit. It is not permissible to say: "These scholars fall within the threat of punishment [related to *khamr*]," because they had an extenuating

---

[132] See, Ibn Mājah, *Sunan*, Kitāb al-Ṭahārah, Bāb al-Nahī 'an Ityān al-Ḥā'iḍ; al-Tirmidhī, *Sunan*, Kitāb Abwāb al-Ṭahārah, Bāb mā Jā' fī Karāhat Ityān al-Ḥā'iḍ.

[133] See, Aḥmad, *Musnad*, 1: 316; Abū Dāwūd, *Sunan*, Kitāb al-Ashribah, Bāb al-'Inab Yu'ṣar li 'l-Khamr; Ibn Mājah, *Sunan*, Kitāb al-Ashribah, Bāb Lu'inat al-Khamr 'alā 'Ashrat Awjuh.

[134] See, al-Bukhārī, *Ṣaḥīḥ*, Kitāb al-Wuḍū', Bāb lā Yajūz al-Wuḍū' bi al-Nabīdh wa lā 'l-Muskir; Muslim, *Ṣaḥīḥ*, Kitāb al-Ashribah, Bāb Bayān ann Kull Muskir Khamr [Every intoxicating drink is prohibited].

[135] See, Muslim, *Ṣaḥīḥ*, Kitāb al-Ashribah, Bāb Bayān ann Kull Muskir Khamr.

[136] See, al-Bukhārī, *Ṣaḥīḥ*, Kitāb al-Ashribah, Bāb al-Khamr min al-'Asal.

reason which they used to form an interpretation, or because of other possible extenuating circumstances. At the same time, it is not permissible to affirm that the drink they consumed was not considered to be a type of *khamr* where the drinker is seriously censured.

The basis of the general statement must incorporate this drinking; there was after all no *khamr* made from grapes in Madīnah. The Prophet (peace be on him) had pronounced *la'n* against the one who sells *khamr*. Some of the Companions sold *khamr* [at the time of 'Umar] and the news of this reached 'Umar (may Allah be pleased with him) who said: "May Allah fight so and so! (*qātala Allāh fulānan*). Does he not know that the Prophet (peace be on him) said: 'Allah condemned [those] Jews to whom it was made prohibited the selling of the fat of the carcass but they melted it and then sold it and made use of its price.'"[137] That particular Companion was not aware of the prohibition of selling *khamr*, yet this did not stop 'Umar (may Allah be pleased with him) from outlining the punishment for this sinful act even though he knew that the person in question was not aware of the prohibition. [He did it] so that that person and others would be discouraged from committing such an act after being made aware of its prohibition.

Furthermore, the Prophet (peace be on him) pronounced *la'n* against the one who squeezed the juice of *khamr* and the one who asked for it to be squeezed. Despite this, many jurists permit a person to squeeze grapes for someone else, even if he knew that his intention is to make *khamr* from it. We have, therefore, an explicit text (*naṣṣ*) regarding the *la'n* upon someone who squeezes grapes [for *khamr*], but it is also known that a person might be excused from the ruling because of the existence of an impediment.

Similarly, there are a number of *ḥadīths* containing the *la'n* of the *wāṣilah* (i.e. the woman who connects extensions to another's hair) and *al-mawṣūlah* (i.e. the woman who sits to have this done to her),[138] but some of the jurists considered it to be only disapproved.

Another example is that the Prophet (peace be on him) said, "He who drinks from a silver vessel is in fact swallowing the fire of Hell down his belly."[139] Yet, again, some of the jurists merely consider this to be strongly disapproved (*karāhat tanzīyhiyyah*).

---

[137] See, al-Bukhārī, *Ṣaḥīḥ*, Kitāb al-Anbyā', Bāb mā Dhukira 'an Banī Isrā'īl; Muslim, *Ṣaḥīḥ*, Kitāb al-Musāqāh, Bāb Taḥrīm Bay' al-Khamr.

[138] See, al-Bukhārī, *Ṣaḥīḥ*, Kitāb al-Libās, Bāb al-Waṣl fī 'l-Sha'r; Muslim, *Ṣaḥīḥ*, Kitāb al-Libās, Bāb Taḥrīm fī 'l-Wāṣilah wa al-Mustawṣilah.

[139] See, al-Bukhārī, *Ṣaḥīḥ*, Kitāb al-Ashribah, Bāb Āniyat al-Fiḍḍah; Muslim, *Ṣaḥīḥ*, Kitāb al-Libās, Bāb Taḥrīm Isti'māl Awānī al-Dhahab wa 'l-Fiḍḍah.

Also it is necessary to act by his statement: "When two Muslims fight each other with their swords, both the killer as well as the slain will enter the Hell-fire"[140] when it comes to the prohibition of two believers fighting each other without just cause. Despite this, we know that the participants in [the battles of] al-Jamal and Ṣiffīn[141] are not people of the fire, as they had extenuating reasons and interpretations justifying the fighting and good deeds which prevented the otherwise necessary cause (*muqtaḍī*) from taking its effect.

The Prophet (peace be on him) said in an authentic *ḥadīth*, "There are three kinds of people with whom Allah will neither speak on the Day of Resurrection, nor look at them, nor purify them [from sins]. They will have a painful chastisement. A person who has more water than he needs and yet he refuses to give it to the traveller; so Allah will say to him on the Day of Judgement: 'Today I will deprive you of My grace, just as you withheld the surplus of that which you did not create yourself;' a person who pledged allegiance to the Imām but for the sake of worldly gain, so that if the Imām bestowed on him something out of that worldly gain, he was satisfied but if he was not given it, he became discontent; and a person who swears a false oath to another person after [the start of the time of] *'aṣr* [prayer] that he was offered a higher price for a commodity than that offered by the second party."[142]

This is a very severe threat to the one who withholds surplus water. Yet there was a group of scholars who permitted such withholding. The existence of such an opinion, however, does not prevent us from believing in the prohibition of this practice on the strength of this *ḥadīth*. Conversely, the existence of this *ḥadīth* does not prevent us from believing that the one who has a reasonable interpretation for the *ḥadīth* [which led him not to act upon it] is excused and is not liable for the punishment stated in that *ḥadīth*.

The Prophet (peace be on him) said, "May Allah reject the *muḥallil* and *muḥallal lahu*."[143] This is an authentic *ḥadīth* narrated from the Messenger of

---

[140] See, al-Bukhārī, *Ṣaḥīḥ*, Kitāb al-Īmān, Bāb wa in Ṭā'ifatān min al-Mu'minīn Iqtatalū; Muslim, *Ṣaḥīḥ*, Kitāb al-Fitan, Bāb idhā Tawājah al-Muslimān bi Sayfayhimā.

[141] See, Aḥmad b. 'Ali Ibn Ḥajar, *al-Iṣābah fī Tamyīz al-Ṣaḥābah* (Beirut: Dār al-Jīl, 1992), 4: 566; 'Abd al-Raḥmān b. Muḥammad Ibn Khaldūn, *Muqaddimah Ibn Khaldūn* (Beirut: Dār al-Qalam, 1984), 213.

[142] See, al-Bukhari, *Ṣaḥīḥ*, Kitāb al-Shahādāt, Bāb al-Yamin ba'd al-'Aṣr; Muslim, *Ṣaḥīḥ*, Kitāb al-Īmān, Bāb Bayān Ghilaẓ Taḥrīm Isbāl al-Izār.

[143] See, Ibn Abī Shaybah, *Muṣannaf*, 7: 292; Abū Dāwūd, *Sunan*, Kitāb al-Nikāḥ, Bāb fī 'l-Taḥlīl; Ibn Mājah, *Sunan*, Kitāb al-Nikāḥ, Bāb al-Muḥallil wa 'l-Muḥallal lahu; Aḥmad b. al-Ḥusayn al-Bayhaqī, *Sunan al-Bayhaqī al-Kubrā* (Makkah: Maktabat Dār al-Bāz, 1994), 7: 208. *Nikāḥ al-Taḥlīl* is a type of marriage performed by a person (*muḥallil*) for the purpose of legitimising the

Allah (peace be on him) and from his Companions (may Allah be pleased with them all) through many channels. However, a group of scholars unreservedly validated the contract of marriage of the *muhallil*.[144] Others validated the contract if the intention to legitimise her remarriage to her previous husband was not stipulated in the contract itself, and they have well-known mitigating factors for concluding with these opinions. This is because the first party [i.e. those who unreservedly validated the above-mentioned contract of marriage], believes that what is in accordance with the general principles is that the contract of marriage does not become invalidated by incorrect conditions, just as it is not invalidated by not knowing one of the two remunerations (*'iwadayn*). Whereas the second party believes that what is in accordance with the general principles is that the conditions which are not stipulated in the contract itself do not affect its validity. It seems this *hadith* did not reach those who held this opinion, as their early works do not mention it. If it had reached them, they would have mentioned it either to act upon it or in response to it. Alternatively, it might have reached them but they interpreted it away, or they thought that it was abrogated or they had some other evidence that opposed it.

Therefore, we know that such people are not liable for this threat, even if they were to commit *tahlil* themselves, believing it to be permissible in that form.

This does not stop us from knowing that *tahlil* is the cause of such punishment [as a general rule], even if it was not to apply with regard to particular individuals because of the absence of a condition or the presence of an impediment.

Finally, there is Mu'āwiyah's (may Allah be pleased with him) claim of kinship with Ziyād ibn Abīh even though he was born from the wedlock of al-Ḥārith b. Kildah, because Abū Sufyān used to say that he was from his own sperm. This was even though the Messenger of Allah (peace be on him) said, "If somebody knowingly claims to be the son of any other than his real father, Paradise will be forbidden to him."[145] He also said, "If somebody claims to be the son of anyone other than his real father, or attributes himself in patronage to other than the one who freed him from slavery, upon him is the *la'n* of Allah and the angels and all people. Allah will neither accept repentance nor

---

remarriage of a man (*muhallal lahu*) to his former wife, from whom she has been divorced thrice and thus irrevocably divorced.

[144] The *muhallil* is the man who marries the divorcee for the purpose of legitimising her remarriage to her previous husband who had irrevocably divorced her.

[145] See, al-Bukhārī, *Ṣaḥīḥ*, Kitāb al-Farā'iḍ, Bāb man Idda'ā ilā Ghayr Abīh; Muslim, *Ṣaḥīḥ*, Kitāb al-Īmān, Bāb man Raghib 'an Abīh.

ransom from him."[146] This is an authentic *ḥadīth*. The Messenger of Allah had, in any case, also ruled that the child is attributed to the husband of the mother, and this is agreed upon.

We know that the one who attributes himself to other than the husband of his mother falls within the threats of punishment stated above; but it is not permissible to single out an individual after the Companions, let alone the Companions themselves, and to say that the threat is incumbent upon him. It is possible that they were not aware of the judgement of the Messenger of Allah (peace be on him) that the child is attributed to the husband, and that they thought that the child must be attributed to the one who caused the pregnancy, and they believed that Abū Sufyān was the one who made Sumayyah, Umm Ziyād, pregnant.

Indeed this ruling might not have been known to many people, especially before the spread of the *Sunnah*, and because it was contrary to the practice in the pre-Islamic period. There might also be other impediments averting the applicability of the threat such as good deeds that erase bad deeds and so on.

This also is a vast subject area. It includes all prohibited matters derived from the Qur'ān and the *Sunnah*, whenever some of the Imāms were not aware of the prohibiting evidence and they saw an act as permissible, or that the prohibiting evidence was opposed, according to them, by other evidence which they considered to be preponderant, and they used their independent reasoning in giving preference to one over the other based on their intellect and knowledge.

Prohibition has implications such as incurring sin, censure, punishment, iniquity [i.e. not meeting what is perceived to be the legal requirements of righteousness in Islam], and so on; but there are conditions and impediments to the applicability of these implications. Prohibitions might sometimes be established but these consequences cannot be applied due to the absence of their conditions or the existence of an impediment, or because the prohibition does not apply to that particular person even though it is established and can be applied to others.

We have only repeated our statements on this issue because the scholars are divided into two camps on this point:

The first: —which is the position held by the majority of the *salaf* and the jurists—is that Allah has only one ruling with regard to any given issue and the one who differs from that position on the basis of an acceptable piece of independent reasoning is mistaken, excused and rewarded. Therefore, the act itself which was committed by the person who had this interpretation is

---

[146] See, Muslim, *Ṣaḥīḥ*, Kitāb al-Ḥajj, Bāb Faḍl al-Madīnah.

prohibited but the implications of prohibition are not applicable to him due to Allah's attribute of forgiveness as He does not charge a soul with more than it can bear.

The second is that the prohibited matter is not considered prohibited for that person, as the prohibiting evidence did not reach him, even though it is considered to be prohibited for others; thus the action itself of that person is not prohibited.

The two opinions are in truth similar, and it is more of a difference in semantics.

This then is what can be said with regard to the *ḥadīths* containing threats where differences exist [among the scholars], i.e. that the scholars are in agreement on the citation of these *ḥadīths* for the prohibition of the action to which the threat is related, regardless of whether they are in agreement or not as to the ruling itself. In fact, in most cases, the need to cite the *ḥadīths* of threat is related to areas of disagreement. They differed, however, in establishing the threat on the basis of such *ḥadīths* where there was nothing definitive available, as we have already mentioned earlier.

And if it was to be asked: why did you not say that *ḥadīths* containing threats cannot be found within the area of dispute, but rather they lie only in the area of agreement, and for every action whose doer is censured or threatened with wrath or punishment, must be interpreted to mean an action whose prohibition is agreed upon, so that those *mujtahids* who acted upon what they thought to be permissible will not be included within the threat of punishment. In fact, the one who believes [in the permissibility] is more serious than the doer; as the former is the one who ordered the latter to do that action, so he is the one who made him liable for the *la'n* or wrath by implication?

We say that the answer can be given in many ways:

The first answer: the ruling of prohibition is either capable of being established where there is disagreement or it is not. If it cannot be established in the event of disagreement, then this necessitates that there be no prohibited matter except one that is agreed upon. As a result every disputed prohibition would become permissible. This is evidently in opposition to the consensus of the *ummah*, and must of necessity be considered invalid in the religion of Islam.

And if prohibitions were to be established despite the presence of disagreement, even if on only one issue, then the *mujtahid* who considered that prohibited action to be permitted would either be liable to the censure and punishment of the one who permits what is prohibited or the one who commits it, or he would not.

Now, whether it is said that he would be liable, or that he would not be liable, then the same will hold true with regard to the established prohibition found in the *ḥadīth* containing a threat, which is agreed upon as well as one which is disputed, as elaborated upon earlier.

In fact the threat is only related to the doer and the punishment for the one who permits what is prohibited is essentially more than that of the punishment for the one who did it without conviction or belief.

Therefore, if it is possible that the prohibition be established, despite there being a dispute, and the *mujtahid* who permitted the action will not be liable for the punishment of making the prohibited permissible because of his an extenuating reason, then it is more appropriate that the doer of the action not be liable for the punishment resulting from that action. Also, as this does not necessitate that the *mujtahid* is included under the effects of this prohibition—such as censure, punishment, etc.—then it equally does not necessitate his inclusion under the threat; a threat is after all no more than a type of censure and punishment. If the inclusion of threat under this type (*jins*) [of censure and punishment] is acceptable, then what was said as an answer for some of its categories is an answer to the others. There is also no benefit in differentiating between the degrees of censure, or how heavy or light the punishment is, because mild censure and punishment in this context is just as problematic as a heavy one; the *mujtahid* is liable to neither the mild nor the heavy censure and punishment. Rather, he is deserving of their opposites, namely reward and recompense.

The second answer: agreement or disagreement with regard to the ruling of an action are matters external to the action itself and its attributes; they are only incidental and occur as a result of lack of knowledge of the issue amongst some of the scholars.

If the general wording (*al-lafẓ al-ʿāmm*) was actually meant to refer to a specific meaning (*al-khāṣṣ*), then there has to be evidence presented to support the specification. This evidence has to come simultaneously with [the general] communication, according to those who do not permit any delay in clarification (*taʾkhīr al-bayān*), or according to the majority of scholars it needs not be chronologically simultaneous, being revealed instead at the time it is needed.

There is no doubt that those who were addressed by a communication at the time of the Messenger of Allah (peace be on him) were in need of knowing the ruling contained in that communication. If the general meaning conveyed by the *laʿn* upon the one who receives *ribā* and the *muḥallil* and other similar cases was intended where there is an agreement upon its prohibition, and yet this [agreement] could not be known except after the death of the Prophet (peace be on him), and the subsequent discussion of the *ummah* upon all the ramifications of that general communication, then that would have meant a postponement in the clarification of the words of the Prophet (peace be on him) until such time. This is [clearly] not acceptable.

The third answer: the *ummah* was addressed by such communication so that it would recognise what is prohibited and avoid it, and will use it as a basis for their consensus, and cite it as evidence when they disagree. If the intention was that prohibition would only be derived from what is agreed upon, then knowledge of the intended meaning would have been dependent on consensus. Its use as evidence, then, would not be valid before the existence of the consensus, but this means it cannot form the basis for a consensus either. This is because the basis for a consensus must exist before it, and therefore it is impossible for the evidence to follow the consensus, as this would lead to an invalid circular argument. Since the people of consensus then will not be able to cite the *ḥadīth* as evidence for any meaning until they know that this meaning is intended, and this cannot be achieved until they have agreement, so the citation depends on the occurrence of the consensus *preceding* it, whilst the consensus depends on the citation of the *ḥadīth*, if indeed the *ḥadīth* was their proof. Therefore, the matter becomes dependent upon itself and thus its existence is impossible, and cannot be an authoritative evidence in the area of disagreement as that evidence simply does not exist. This creates a suspension of the use of *ḥadīth* to indicate rulings in areas of agreement and disagreement. The [inevitable] consequence of this is that none of the texts which refer to the gravity of an action can also inform us of the prohibition of that action, and this must be absolutely invalid.

The fourth answer: this requires that none of these *ḥadīth*s can be relied upon unless it is known that the *ummah* agreed on a given meaning for them. Therefore, it would not have been permissible for the first generation (*al-ṣadr al-awwal*) to have used these *ḥadīth*s as evidence. In fact, those who heard these *ḥadīth*s directly from the Messenger of Allah (peace be on him) would not be allowed to cite them as evidence. It would have been obligatory upon a person, who hears such a *ḥadīth* and finds that many scholars had acted upon it and finds no opposition to it, not to act upon it until he is satisfied that there is nobody opposing it anywhere in the world. It is also not allowed for him to cite consensus upon an issue until he carries out a similarly thorough investigation.

This will lead to the invalidity of the citation of a *ḥadīth* of the Messenger of Allah (peace be on him) by the mere existence of one *mujtahid* holding an opposing opinion. As a result, the opinion of one person validates and invalidates the words of the Messenger of Allah (peace be on him).

If that person happened to be mistaken, then his mistake will have invalidated the words of the Messenger of Allah (peace be on him). This is known to be void by necessity; because if it were to be said that a *hadīth* cannot be cited except after knowing the existence of a consensus upon it, then this leads to the implications of texts becoming dependent upon consensus, and yet this is in opposition to consensus! If it were to be true, there would be no meaning to be derived from texts, as only consensus would have relevance, whereas texts would have no significance.

If, on the other hand, it were to be said that it should be cited as evidence solely on the basis that a conflicting opinion is not known, then this would still result in the opinion of one person within this *ummah* invalidating the implication of a text, and this too is in opposition to consensus and is invalid by necessity in Islam.

The fifth answer: is that either the belief of the entire *ummah* in the prohibition is stipulated for a communication to be comprehensive, or the belief of the scholars alone regarding that prohibition is sufficient.

If the first were correct, then it would not be permissible to cite the *hadīths* on threats as evidence for prohibition until it was known that the entire *ummah*—even those who were brought up in the most isolated valleys and those who recently converted to Islam—believed that the prohibition exists. No Muslim can claim this, nor indeed any sane person, because knowledge subjected to this condition is practically impossible.

If it were to be said that the belief of all scholars in the prohibition is sufficient, the response would be that the consensus of the scholars was made a condition out of fear that the threat of punishment might encompass some of the *mujtahid*s, even where they were only mistaken. This is akin to the layman who did not hear the prohibiting evidence, as fear of this person's falling under the *la'n* is similar to the fear of a *mujtahid* falling under it.

This argument cannot be dismissed by saying that the *mujtahid* in question is among the loftiest and most righteous of this *ummah*, whereas that person is on the fringe of and one of the laymen of this *ummah*; the difference in their status does not necessitate that they be excluded from the ruling. This is because just as Allah (the Exalted) forgives the *mujtahid* when he makes an honest mistake, He also forgives the mistake of an unlearned one who was unable to learn. In fact, the mischief resulting from a layman committing a prohibited act, which he was not aware of and which it was not possible for him to know, is far less than the harm resulting from some of the Imāms permitting that which has been prohibited by the Lawgiver, through lack of awareness of the prohibition as well as the incapability of knowing it. For this reason it was said, "Beware of the lapse of the scholar, for when he slips a whole community slips as a result."[147] [On this subject] Ibn 'Abbās (may Allah be pleased with them both) said, "Woe to the scholar from those who follow him."[148]

Thus, if the mistake of a scholar can be pardoned, despite the enormity of the harm caused by his action, then it is more appropriate that a layman be forgiven, since the harm caused by his action is less severe.

Granted, they are different from another aspect, namely that the *mujtahid* has based his opinion on *ijtihād* and the harm caused by his mistake is buried within his account of good deeds accumulated through the dissemination of knowledge and revival of the *Sunnah*. Allah has differentiated between them in this respect so he rewarded the *mujtahid* for his *ijtihād* and the scholar for his knowledge and this reward was not shared with the ignorant lay persons. Therefore, they are equal with regard to forgiveness but dissimilar with regard to reward. Punishing someone who does not deserve punishment is inconceivable, regardless of whether he is noble or lowly. Therefore, ruling out this possibility of punishment in the context of a *ḥadīth* should be understood in a way that includes both parties [i.e. both scholar and layman].

The sixth answer: among the *ḥadīth*s on threat there are those that are explicit texts on the disputed issue, such as "the *la'n* of the *muḥallal lahu*."[149] Some scholars say that this person could not possibly incur any sin as he was not an integral part of the first marriage contract, so how is it possible to say that he was condemned due to his *belief* that it is obligatory to fulfil the *taḥlīl* contract? Hence, whoever believes that the contract of marriage for the first person (i.e. the *muḥallil*) is valid, even if the condition attached to it is invalid, then the remarriage by the second (i.e. the *muḥallal lahu*) must be permissible. This scholar, therefore, does not believe that the second person has committed a sin.

And even the *muḥallil* is either condemned because of the act of *taḥlīl* or because of his belief that it is obligatory to fulfil the condition attached to the contract, or because of both reasons. If it is the first or the third reason then the intent of the *ḥadīth* has been achieved. If it is the second, then this *belief* is the cause of the *la'n* regardless of whether there was a contract of *taḥlīl* or not. This would mean that what is mentioned in the *ḥadīth* would not be the actual reason for the *la'n* and the actual reason for the *la'n* was not mentioned in the

---

[147] 'Abd Allāh ibn al-Mubārak al-Marwizī, *al-Zuhd* (Beirut: Dār al-Kutub al-'Ilmiyyah, n.d.), 1: 520.

[148] See, Aḥmad b. al-Ḥusayn al-Bayhaqī, *al-Madkhal ilā al-Sunan al-Kubrā* (Kuwait: Dār al-Khulafā' li 'l-Kitāb, 1404), 445.

[149] *Muḥallal lahu* is the husband of a woman who divorces her thrice, after which another man who marries her solely for the purpose of legitimising her remarriage to him.

ḥadīth and this is not acceptable. If the person who believed in the necessity of fulfilling the *taḥlīl* contract was ignorant [of the law] there is no *la'n* upon him. If he knew that it is not obligatory, then he could not believe in its obligation, except if he was an opponent of the Messenger of Allah (peace be on him) and he would then be a disbeliever, and then the *ḥadīth*'s *la'n* would be related to the *la'n* upon disbelievers. But disbelief is not linked to the denial of this minor ruling alone. This would be akin to saying: "Allah has rejected the one who disbelieves in the Messenger's ruling that the stipulation of divorce in a contract of marriage is invalid."

This is a general statement in both wording and meaning and it is spontaneous generality (*'umūm al-mubtada'*). It is not permissible to link such generality to an unusual ramification, lest the statement be considered as including incorrect linguistic usage or suggest an incapability of expression similar to one who interprets the Prophet's saying, "Any woman who marries without the permission of her guardian, then her marriage is invalid"[150] as being related only to the *mukātabah*.[151]

And to clarify the unusual nature of this interpretation [in the context of the *ḥadīth* on *taḥlīl*] it would mean that the ignorant Muslim would not be included within this *ḥadīth* nor the Muslim who knows that it is not obligatory to fulfil this condition[152] and he does not stipulate it in the contract believing that its [fulfilment] is an obligation except if he was a disbeliever, and the disbeliever does not marry in the way Muslims do, unless if he was a hypocrite. Marriages that occur in this manner are very rare occurrences. Indeed, it would be right to suggest that such a meaning is unlikely to have occurred in the mind of the speaker when the *ḥadīth* was uttered.

We have cited many evidences in other places on the fact that this *ḥadīth* is meant to address the *muḥallil* who intended his action even if he did not stipulate it in the contract itself.

The same is true also with regard to specified threats, such as *la'n* and the fire and the like, which were explicitly stated in the texts even though disagreement clearly remains. For instance, there is the *ḥadīth* of Ibn 'Abbās (may Allah be pleased with him) from the Prophet (peace be on him) that he said, "May Allah reject the female visitors to the graves and those who build

---

[150] See, 'Abd al-Razzāq, *Muṣannaf*, 6: 195; Ibn Abī Shaybah, *Muṣannaf*, 3: 454; Aḥmad, *Musnad*, 6: 66, Abū Dāwūd, *Sunan*, Kitāb al-Nikāḥ, Bāb fī 'l-Walī; Ibn Mājah, *Sunan*, Kitāb al-Nikāḥ, Bāb lā Nikāḥ illā bi Walī.

[151] The *mukātabah* is a slave who ratifies a contract of emancipation to free herself in return for instalments attaining complete freedom upon completion of the agreed payment. See, Ibn Manẓūr, *Lisān al-'Arab*, 1: 700.

[152] I. e. to divorce the wife after ratifying the marriage to wave the way for her previous husband to remarry her after divorcing her triply.

mosques and [place] lamps on graves."[153] Al-Tirmidhī said that this is a *hasan hadīth*.[154] Yet, the visitation of graves by women was allowed by some scholars, and disapproved —not prohibited—by others.

Another example is that of 'Uqbah b. 'Āmir (may Allah be pleased with him) on the authority of the Prophet (peace be on him) who said "May Allah reject those who have anal intercourse with women."[155]

There is the *hadīth* of Anas (may Allah be pleased with him) from the Prophet (peace be on him), in which he said, "The importer (of commodities) is blessed and the monopolist is rejected."[156]

We have already mentioned the following *hadīth*: "The three persons to whom Allah would neither speak on the Day of Resurrection, nor look at them, nor purify them (from sins), and they will have a painful chastisement ..."[157] Among them is one who refuses to give the surplus water in his possession to one who needs it.

Similarly, "the one who sells *khamr* is rejected"[158] whereas some of the early people sold it.

Also, it is established as authentic from more than one channel that the Prophet (peace be him) said: "Allah will not look at the one who trails his garment on the ground out of pride."[159] The Prophet also said, "There are three whom Allah will not speak to, look at, or praise on the Day of Judgement and theirs will be a painful punishment: the one who wears his garment below his ankles, the one who reminds others of his favours, and the one who sells his product by means of making false oaths."[160] [This] despite some jurists' stating that wearing the garment below the ankles and trailing the garment on the ground out of pride are disapproved and not prohibited.

---

[153] See, Ibn Abī Shaybah, *Muṣannaf*, 2: 151, Aḥmad, *Musnad*, 1: 229; Abū Dāwūd, *Sunan*, Kitāb al-Kharāj, Bāb fī Ziyārat al-Nisā' li 'l-Qubūr; al-Tirmidhī, *Sunan*, Kitāb Abwāb al-Ṣalāt, Bāb mā Jā' fī Karāhiyat an Yutakhadh 'alā 'l-Qabr Masjid; al-Nasā'ī, *al-Sunan al-Kubrā*, Kitāb al-Janā'iz, Bāb al-Taghlīẓ fī Itikhādh al-Suruj 'alā 'l-Qubūr.

[154] Al-Tirmidhī, *Sunan*, Kitāb Abwāb al-Ṣalāt, Bāb mā Jā' fī Karāhiyat an Yutakhadh 'alā 'l-Qabr Masjid.

[155] See, Aḥmad, *Musnad*, 2: 479; Abū Dāwūd, *Sunan*, Kitāb al-Nikāḥ, Bāb fī Jāmi' al-Nikāḥ; al-Nasā'ī, *al-Sunan al-Kubrā*, Kitāb 'Ishrat al-Nisā', Bāb Dhikr Ikhtilāf Alfāẓ al-Nāqilīn li Khabar Abī Hurayrah.

[156] See, 'Abd al-Razzāq, *Muṣannaf*, 8: 204.

[157] See n. 142 above.

[158] See n. 133 above.

[159] See, al-Bukhārī, *Ṣaḥīḥ*, Kitāb Faḍā'il al-Ṣaḥabah, Bāb Qawl al-Nabī law kunt Muttakhidhan Khalīlā; Muslim, *Ṣaḥīḥ*, Kitāb al-Libās, Bāb Karāhat mā Zād 'alā 'l-Ḥajah min al-Firāsh wa 'l-Libās.

[160] See, Muslim, *Ṣaḥīḥ*, Kitāb al-Īmān, Bāb Bayān Ghilaẓ Taḥrīm Isbāl al-Izār.

Similarly, there is his [i.e. the Prophet's] saying (peace be on him), "Allah has rejected *al-wāṣilah* and *al-mawṣūlah*"[161] and this is one of the most authentic *ḥadīths*. And there is well-known disagreement over the extensions of the hair.

Finally, there is his [i.e. the Prophet's] statement (peace be on him), "He who drinks out of silver utensils is only filling his abdomen with Hell Fire"[162] while some of the scholars did not deem this to be a prohibition.

The seventh answer: the reason necessitating generality is present whereas the aforementioned opposite is not deemed as acceptable because, taken to its logical conclusion, it would mean its application in issues of agreement and disagreement and this will lead to the inclusion, within the threat of punishment, of some who do not deserve to be included.

The response to this is that if the particularisation [of a ruling] is against the norm, then its multiplication (*takthīruhu*) (i.e. by the inclusion of other than those who were intended to be included under it) stands against the norm. As a result the one who is excused for his ignorance, or *ijtihād*, or imitation (*taqlīd*), he is exempt from the generality of the text. On the other hand, the ruling includes those who were not excused, in the way that it includes the issues of agreement. This [type] of particularisation (i.e. the exemption of some people from the generality of the text because they were excused) is less and therefore it is more deserving to be accepted (*awlā*).

The eighth answer: if we were to understand the text in accordance with this, then it would have contained mention of the reason for the *laʿn* and the ruling would hence not apply to the exception because of the existence of an impediment. There is no doubt that the one who promises or issues a threat, does not have to specifically mention those who are exempted because of the existence of an impediment. Therefore, the statement will continue to be consistent with the proper methodology.

If, however, we were to associate the rejection (*laʿn*) with committing an act the prohibition of which is agreed upon, or we made the holding of a belief opposing consensus as the reason for the *laʿn*, then that reason is not mentioned in the *ḥadīth*. Moreover, that generality in the text has to be specified. If specification is a must in both cases, then it is more appropriate to apply it in the first case because of its agreement with the correct methodology and the absence of implication of a missing syntactical part (*iḍmār*).

The ninth answer: the reason behind this claim is to negate the inclusion in the *laʿn* of the one who is excused. We have already mentioned that the intention behind the *ḥadīths* containing a threat is to make clear that the act in question is a cause for that *laʿn*, so the implicit statement is as follows: "this act

---

[161] See n. 139 above.

[162] See n. 139 above.

is a reason for the *la'n*." This does not, however, necessitate the fulfilment of the ruling upon every person, although it does bring about the existence of the cause without its implication and there is nothing objectionable in this.

We have already established that there is no censure for the *mujtahid* to the extent that we say: the one who permits the prohibited act incurs more sin than the doer of that act, but despite this we say that the one who has an extenuating reason is excused.

And if it were to be asked: who is to be punished seeing as the doer of this prohibited matter is either a *mujtahid* or someone who follows him (*muqallid lahu*) and neither of them are included under the punishment? We will say: the answer has different aspects:

The first aspect: the aim of the text is to clarify that this act necessitates punishment regardless of whether someone actually commits that act or not.

If it were assumed that every doer of that act is lacking the [requisite] conditions for the punishment or there is an impediment that prevents the application of the punishment, then this would not negate the forbidden quality of the act. Rather, we will know that it is prohibited and [it is hoped] that whoever knows of the prohibition will refrain from it. The existence of excuses for the one who commits a prohibited act is something bestowed from Allah's Mercy.

This is similar to the principle that minor prohibited acts are prohibited even though they can be expiated for [by the commission of certain good deeds]—provided that the major prohibited acts are avoided. This is the case with all acts on which there is dispute regarding their prohibition. When it is clear that they are prohibited, even though the one who does so on the basis of *ijtihād* or imitation might be excused, this does not stop us from believing in their prohibition.

The second aspect: the clarification of a ruling is a reason for the removal of any doubts which prevent the applicability of the punishment. This is because an excuse based on the [mistaken] belief is not meant to last forever; rather, the aim is for doubts to be removed if at all possible. If this was not the case then the clarification of knowledge would not have been obligatory, it would have been better to leave the people in their ignorance, and it would have been better for them to disregard the evidence available in disputed issues rather than seek to clarify them.

The third aspect: the clarification of the ruling and the threat support the one who has abstained from committing the prohibited act in remaining with firm resolve. If it were not [for the clarification of the ruling and the threat] the commission of such acts would become widespread.

The fourth aspect: that an excuse cannot be considered as an excuse except where one is unable to remove it. Therefore, whenever it is possible for a person to know the truth and he falls short, he is not to be excused.

The fifth aspect: some people who commit the [prohibited] act might perhaps exercise an *ijtihād* which falls short of the *ijtihād* that would permit that action to the person or an imitator whose imitation was not of a standard that could make the action permissible for him. Therefore, this kind of example has within it a cause for the applicability of the threat without the existence of this specific impediment. As a result, he will be liable to the threat and he will be subjected to it, unless another impediment was to be found for him, such as repentance or good deeds which erase bad deeds, and so on.

Then again, this is problematic, because the person might think that his *ijtihād* or imitation permits him to do what he did and he could be right sometimes and mistaken at other times. If, however, he sought the truth and did not leave it to his desires, then Allah does not charge a soul with more than it can bear.

The tenth answer: [i.e. to the claim that the *ḥadīth*s containing threats are related to the issues of agreement only]: Whilst understanding these *ḥadīth*s upon their required meanings leads to the inclusion of some *mujtahid*s within the scope of the threat, giving some other meaning may similarly lead to the inclusion of some *mujtahid*s within it. Therefore, if the inclusion is unavoidable in both cases, then the *ḥadīth* is free of opposing evidence and as a result it is obligatory to implement it.

To clarify this: many imāms stated that the doer of a disputed act is blameworthy, among them being ʿAbd Allāh ibn ʿUmar (may Allah be pleased with him). When he was asked about the one who marries a woman to legitimise her subsequent remarriage to her previous husband, while she and her previous husband were not aware of [his intention], he said: "This is fornication and not marriage. May Allah reject the *muḥallil* and the *muḥallal lahu*."[163] This is narrated from him through more than one channel. It is also narrated from others, among them Imām Aḥmad ibn Ḥanbal (may Allah have mercy upon him) who said, "If he seeks to legitimise remarriage to a previous husband, then he is a *muḥallil*, and he is rejected."[164] This sort of opinion has been narrated from groups of the imāms in many issues of disagreement, such as *khamr*, usury and the like.

---

[163] See, Abū Dāwūd, *Sunan*, Kitāb al-Nikāḥ, Bāb fī 'l-Taḥlīl; Ibn Mājah, *Sunan*, Kitāb al-Nikāḥ, Bāb al-Muḥallil wa al-Muḥallal lah; Ibn Abī Shaybah, *Muṣannaf*, 7: 292; Yūsuf b. ʿAbd Allāh Ibn ʿAbd al-Barr, *al-Tamhīd li mā fī 'l-Mawaṭṭa' min Maʿānī wa 'l-Asānīd* (Beirut: Dār al-Kutub al-ʿIlmiyyah, 1999), 13: 235.

[164] See, Ibn Qudāmah, *al-Mughnī*, 7: 138.

If the *shar'i la'n* and the other forms of threat do not apply except in issues of agreement, then this would mean that these scholars have pronounced rejection (*la'n*) against someone who is not permitted to have a *la'n* pronounced against them and consequently they deserve the threat which was narrated in several *ḥadīths* such as the statement of the Prophet (peace be on him): "Pronouncing *la'n* against the Muslim is the same as killing him"[165] and his statement (peace be on him) in the narration of Ibn Mas'ūd (may Allah be pleased with him) that, "Insulting the Muslim is iniquity and fighting him is disbelief."[166] These are agreed upon *ḥadīths*.

It is narrated from Abū 'l-Dardā' (may Allah be pleased with him) that he heard the Messenger of Allah (peace be on him) say: "Verily, insulters and those who pronounce *la'n* will not be given the right of intercession on the Day of Judgement nor will they be accepted as witnesses."[167]

And it is narrated from Abū Hurayrah (may Allah be pleased with him) that the Messenger of Allah (peace be on him) said: "It is not appropriate for one who is very truthful to pronounce *la'n*."[168] [Imām] Muslim narrates both of these two *ḥadīths*.

And it is narrated from 'Abd Allāh ibn Mas'ūd (may Allah be pleased with him) that the Messenger of Allah (peace be on him) said: "The believer is not an insulter, nor does he pronounce *la'n*, nor is he indecent, nor shameless."[169] This is narrated by al-Tirmidhī, who said that it is a *ḥasan ḥadīth*.[170]

And in another narration [Prophet (peace be on him) said]: "No person pronounces *la'n* against something which does not deserve it except that the *la'n* will rebound upon him."[171]

So this is the threat which accompanies this type of *la'n*, to the extent that it is said that whoever pronounces *la'n* against one who is undeserving of it, he will in turn receive *la'n*, and this kind of *la'n* is an iniquity that takes away truthfulness, the right of intercession, and being a witness [on the Day of Judgement]. This [as mentioned earlier] applies to the one who pronounces *la'n* against one who does not deserve it.

---

[165] See, al-Bukhārī, *Ṣaḥīḥ*, Kitāb al-Adab, Bāb man Akfar Akhāh bi Ghayr Ta'wīl; Muslim, *Ṣaḥīḥ*, Kitāb al-Īmān, Bāb Ghilaẓ Taḥrīm Qatl al-Insān Nafsah.

[166] See, al-Bukhārī, *Ṣaḥīḥ*, Kitāb al-Īmān, Bāb Khawf al-Mu'min min an Yaḥbaṭa 'Amaluh; Muslim, *Ṣaḥīḥ*, Kitāb al-Īmān, Bāb Ghilaẓ Taḥrīm Qatl al-Insān Nafsah.

[167] See, Muslim, *Ṣaḥīḥ*, Kitāb al-Birr wa 'l-Ṣilah, Bāb al-Nahy 'an La'n al-Dawāb wa Ghayrihā.

[168] See, ibid.

[169] See, Ibn Abī Shaybah, *Muṣannaf*, 6: 162; Aḥmad, *Musnad*, 1: 404.

[170] See, al-Tirmidhī, *Sunan*, Kitāb al-Birr wa 'l-Ṣilah, Bāb mā Jā' fī 'l-La'nah.

[171] See, Abū Dāwūd, *Sunan*, Kitāb al-Adab, Bāb fī 'l-La'n.

Therefore, if the one who commits a disputed act is not included in the purview of the source text, then he does not deserve it and the one who pronounces *la'n* against him will be liable to this other threat. This would mean that those *mujtahids* who considered issues of dispute to fall within the ambit of the *ḥadīth* would be liable to this threat.

Therefore, if that which is feared can exist regardless of the presence or otherwise of a dispute, then it will be known that it is in fact not to be feared, and nothing can impede the use of the *ḥadīths* as evidence.

However, if the feared possibility is not found in either of the two possibilities (i.e. the disagreed upon issue or agreed upon issue) then this means that the feared possibility does not exist at all

That is so because when inseparability (*talāzum*) is established and it is known that they (i.e. the *mujtahids*) are included within the scope of a threat in issues of disagreement, it necessitates that they also fall within it in the absence of disagreement. Thus, one of two matters must be affirmed, that is either the existence of the cause and the effect which would mean they are all included or the non-existence of the cause and effect which would mean their exclusion as a whole. This is because whenever the cause exists, so too does its effect and conversely, whenever the cause is non-existent, so too is the effect.

This is enough to refute the counter-argument. Our belief, however, is that the reality is that *mujtahids* are not included under either of the two possibilities as we have just clarified. This is because to fall within the scope of a threat, there must be no mitigating factors present in the commission of an act. The one who has a *shar'ī* excuse is not included within a threat under any circumstances. Likewise, the *mujtahid* is excused. Indeed, he is rewarded. A necessary condition for inclusion within a threat is therefore absent in his case and as a result he cannot fall within its ambit whether he believes that the *ḥadīth* must be interpreted according to its apparent meaning, or whether there is some dispute in this regard, for which he is excused. And this is a devastating implication (of their argument) (*ilzām mufḥim*) which cannot be avoided except through one argument, which is to say: I accept that among the *mujtahid* scholars there are those who believe that issues of dispute can still be included within the texts pertaining to threat, and they therefore utilise threats in such issues of disputes on the basis of that belief, so they would, for instance, pronounces *la'n* against the one who did the action in question. Nevertheless, they are mistaken in this belief, although this is a mistake for which they are excused and [instead] rewarded [for their *ijtihād*].

As a result, they would not be included within the purview of the threat regarding the one who pronounces *la'n* against another without legitimate reason. This is because such a threat, according to me, is related only to the *la'n*, the prohibition of which is agreed upon. Therefore, whoever utters a *la'n* the prohibition of which is agreed upon, he has exposed himself to the aforementioned threat. If the *la'n* is, however, a disputed issue, it will not be included in the *ḥadīths* of threat just as an action which is the subject of dispute as to its permissibility or the permissibility of pronouncing *la'n* against its doer is not included within the *ḥadīths* containing such threats.

Therefore, just as I exclude the issues of dispute from the first threat I should also exclude the issues of dispute from being included under the second threat, and I also should believe that the *ḥadīths* containing threats in both cases do not cover disputed issues, neither with regard to the permissibility of the action nor the permissibility of pronouncing *la'n* against its doer whether he held the action to be permissible or prohibited. In fact, I do not, in either case, permit pronouncing *la'n* against the doer of the action or pronouncing *la'n* against the one who pronounces *la'n* against the doer, nor do I believe that the doer or the imprecator falls within a *ḥadīth* containing a threat. I would not be harsh on the one who pronounces *la'n* in the manner of one who thought he was liable to the threat of punishment; rather, I consider his *la'n* upon the doer of a disputed act to be an issue of *ijtihād*. I do, however, believe he was wrong in his imprecation just as I might believe that the one who permitted the disputed action is also mistaken, as there are three opinions with regard to such disputed issues:

First: to hold that it is permissible.

Second: to believe in the prohibition and the applicability of the threat.

Third: to hold that it is prohibited but without such a strong threat of punishment being applicable.

I am inclined to favour this third opinion due to the existence of evidence for the prohibition of the action, but also for the prohibition of pronouncing *la'n* against the one who commits a disputed action, coupled with my belief that the narrated *ḥadīths* on threatening the doer of an act and the imprecator do not seem to imply these two cases.

So it could be said to the interlocutor: if you were to allow the *la'n* directed at the one who commits this act to be considered among the issues of *ijtihād*, then it would also be allowed to use the apparent text as evidence for this. There would then be no avoiding the possibility that disputed issues were intended to be included within the *ḥadīths* of threat, and what necessitates it to be intended exists and therefore it must be acted upon. If, however, you did not allow the *la'n* of this doer to be considered among the issues of *ijtihād* then this *la'n* is definitely prohibited. There is no doubt that the one who pronounces *la'n* against a *mujtahid* with a *la'n* that is prohibited with absolute certainty would fall within the narrated threat upon the imprecator, even if he did this on the basis of an interpretation, as is the case with the one who pronounced *la'n* against some of the righteous *salaf*.

Therefore, a circular argument is created whether you were convinced of the prohibition of pronouncing *la'n* against the doer of a disputed act, or you allowed the difference of opinion on this. Your aforementioned belief does not prevent adducing texts pertaining to threats in either case, and this should be clear.

And it can also be said to him (i.e. the objector): our purpose in this argument is not to affirm the applicability of such threats to issues of disagreement, but merely to allow for the use of such *ḥadīths* pertaining to threat as evidence within such issues of disagreement. Such *ḥadīths* can indicate two rulings: (1) the prohibition of the act itself; and (2) the threat. What you have mentioned deals only with negating the *ḥadīths*' reference to the threat. Our aim here is to clarify its implications for the prohibition. Therefore, if you were to insist that the *ḥadīths* condemning the imprecator do not treat those *la'n* that are disputed, then no evidence would remain for the prohibition of such disputed *la'n*. As we have mentioned, we are discussing such disputed *la'n*, and if they are not prohibited then they must be permissible.

Or it could be said: if there is no evidence for its prohibition, it is not permissible to believe in its prohibition and yet that which necessitates such permissibility [i.e. to believe in its prohibition] is established through the *ḥadīths* cursing those who did the action. Moreover, the scholars disagreed over the permissibility of cursing him, but there is no evidence prohibiting such cursing according to this. Therefore it is obligatory to act upon the evidence indicating the permissibility of cursing him because there is nothing to oppose this evidence. This renders the question void.

There is also circularity in the argument on the part of the interlocutor from another perspective. This is that the majority of the texts prohibiting imprecation contain threats themselves. If the citation of a text containing a threat [of cursing] in matters of disagreement is not permissible then it cannot be permissible to cite them as evidence for a *la'n* upon one who commits a disputed action, as we have clarified earlier.

If the interlocutor were to say, "I cite consensus for the prohibition of this *la'n*," it will be said to him that consensus has only been established for the prohibition of pronouncing *la'n* against a specific individual who is named from amongst those of outstanding virtue, whereas you are aware of the disagreement concerning the *la'n* upon a generic attribute or characteristic that may be found in some people [without naming a particular individual]. It was mentioned earlier that cursing a characteristic does not mean its application to every individual case, unless the conditions for it are fulfilled and there are no impediments, and this is not the case here.

It can also be said to him that all the evidences mentioned earlier indicating the impermissibility of restricting these *ḥadīth*s to issues upon which there is agreement can be used here, and they undermine this counter-argument just as they undermine the original question.

This is not, however, an example of using evidence as a premise amongst the premises for another evidence, so that it could be argued that this is actually only one evidence despite the prolongation (*al-taṭwīl*); because the intention is to clarify that the feared outcome which they thought existed, can be found in both cases (agreement and disagreement); therefore it should not be considered a feared outcome and as a result it is one evidence that has indicated that issues of dispute are included, and that there is no problem with that.

It is not also objectionable that the evidence for one issue is used as a premise in evidence for another issue, even if the two issues are closely intertwined.

The eleventh answer: the scholars are in agreement on the obligation of acting upon the *ḥadīth*s containing a threat to the extent that they imply a prohibition. Some of them only disagreed specifically with regard to the establishment of threats on the basis of *ḥadīth* narrated in isolated *isnāds* (*āḥād*) containing such threats, whereas there is no credible or significant disagreement on affirming prohibitions based on *āḥād ḥadīth*. Indeed, it was the habit of the scholars among the Companions and their followers and the jurists after them (may Allah be pleased with them all) in their letters and treatises to cite *āḥād ḥadīth* in issues of disagreement and other issues. In fact, if a *ḥadīth* contains a threat, this is stronger in emphasising the prohibition, as this would normally be understood by the intellect from such statements.

Also, we have already indicated the preference for the opinion of those who act upon them [*āḥād ḥadīth*s] in rulings and believe in the threats contained within them, and that this is the opinion of the majority of scholars. No argument can, therefore, be accepted which contradicts an opinion agreed upon by the scholars.

The twelfth answer: the texts containing such threats within the Qur'ān and the *Sunnah* are abundant, and to base opinions upon them must be considered obligatory in general and absolute terms without specifying individual culprits. Thus, it could be said that "this is rejected" or "the object of wrath" or "liable for the hellfire," especially if the actual person in question were to possess virtue[s'] and good deeds. This is because all humans other than the Prophets (peace be on them all) are capable of committing minor and major sins, whilst that person might remain a *ṣiddīq* (an extremely truthful person) or *shahīd* (a martyr) or righteous as a consequence of the effects of a sin—as mentioned earlier—being nullified through repentance, seeking forgiveness, good deeds erasing bad ones, trials and tribulations expiating sins, intercession, or simply through the Will and Mercy of Allah.

So when we affirm what is necessitated by the statement of Allah (The Exalted): ❨*Those who unjustly consume the property of orphans, are actually swallowing Fire into their own bellies: They will be enduring a Blazing Fire!*❩;[172] and ❨*But those who disobey Allah and His Messenger and transgress His limits will be admitted to a Fire, and there they will stay: And they shall have a humiliating punishment*❩;[173] and ❨*O you who believe! Do not wrongfully consume each other's wealth but trade by mutual consent: do not kill each other, for verily Allah is Merciful to you! If any of you does these things, out of hostility and injustice, we shall make him suffer the Fire: that is easy for Allah*❩[174] and other verses containing a threat or when we speak about what is necessitated by the statements of the Prophet (peace be on him), "May Allah reject the one who drinks *khamr*"[175] or "the one who is recalcitrant toward his parents, or changes the landmarks of the land"[176] or "May Allah reject the thief"[177] or "may Allah reject the one who takes *ribā*, the one who gives it, and the two witnesses and the scribe"[178] or "may Allah reject the one who does not pay his *zakāt* or exceeds the boundaries in this regard"[179] or "he who introduces any innovations [in religion] in Madīnah, or gives a shelter to someone who committed a crime, Allah's *la‘n* is upon him, as well as that of the angels and all the people"[180] or "the one who trails his garment on the ground out of pride, Allah will not look at him on the day of judgement"[181] or "He who has

---

[172] Qur'ān 4: 10.

[173] Qur'ān 4: 14.

[174] Qur'ān 4: 29–30.

[175] See n. 133 above.

[176] See, Muslim, *Ṣaḥīḥ*, Kitāb al-Aḍāḥi, Bāb Taḥrīm al-Dhabḥ li Ghayr Allāh Ta‘ālā.

[177] See, al-Bukhārī, *Ṣaḥīḥ*, Kitāb al-Ḥudūd, Bāb La‘n al-Sāriq idhā lam Yusam; Muslim, *Ṣaḥīḥ*, Kitāb al-Ḥudūd, Bāb Ḥadd al-Sāriqah.

[178] See note 125 above.

[179] See, ‘Abd al-Razzāq, *Muṣannaf*, 6: 269; Ibn Abī Shaybah, *Muṣannaf*, 2: 354; Ibn Khuzaymah, *al-Ṣaḥīḥ*, 4: 8; al-Bayhaqī, *al-Sunan al-Kubrā*, 4: 82.

[180] See, al-Bukhārī, *Ṣaḥīḥ*, Kitāb al-Ḥajj, Bāb Ḥaram al-Madīnah; Muslim, *Ṣaḥīḥ*, Kitāb al-Ḥajj, Bāb Faḍl al-Madīnah.

[181] See n. 158 above.

in his heart the weight of a mustard seed of pride will not enter Paradise"[182] or "He who acts dishonestly towards us is not of us"[183] or "If somebody claims to be the son of any other than his real father, or attributes himself to other than the one who freed him from slavery, will not enter Paradise"[184] or "He who swore a false oath in order to entitle himself [to possess] a property, will meet Allah in a state that [Allah] would be angry with him"[185] or "He who appropriates the right of a Muslim by swearing a false oath, Allah would make Hell-fire necessary for him and would declare Paradise forbidden for him"[186] or "The one who severs the ties of kinship will not enter Paradise"[187] and other such *hadīths* containing such threats, it is not permissible to single out a particular person from among those who committed these actions and to say that the relevant threat has befallen that person. This is because of the possibility of repentance and other ways of removing the punishment.

It would also not be permissible to say that this (i.e. the existence of such *hadīths*) necessitates pronouncing rejection (*la'n*) against Muslims or the *ummah* of the Prophet Muḥammad (peace be on him) or pronouncing *la'n* against the *ṣiddīqīn* or the upright ones. This is because it might be that whenever the upright righteous one commits one of those prohibited actions, there would no doubt be an impediment preventing the applicability of the punishment to him, despite the cause of the punishment being present.

Hence, whoever did these actions thinking that they were permissible—either on the basis of *ijtihād*, imitation or other similar reasons—the last resort is that he is from a class of the righteous from whom the threat was lifted through an impediment, just as the threat might be impeded by repentance, good deeds which erase the bad ones, and other such reasons.

Note that this is the path that must be adopted [with regard to this matter], as there are only two ugly alternatives to this:

The first: to assert the applicability of the threat to each and every individual [committing the act] with the argument that this is merely acting upon what is necessitated by the texts.

---

[182] See, Muslim, *Ṣaḥīḥ*, Kitāb al-Īmān, Bāb Taḥrīm al-Kibr.

[183] See, Muslim, *Ṣaḥīḥ*, Kitāb al-Īmān, Bāb Qawl al-Nabī man Ghashshanā fa laysa Minnā.

[184] See n. 145 above.

[185] See, al-Bukhārī, *Ṣaḥīḥ*, Kitāb al-Shahādāt, Bāb Qawl Allāh Ta'ālā inna 'l-ladhīn Yashtarūna bi 'Ahd Allāh; Muslim, *Ṣaḥīḥ*, Kitāb al-Īmān, Bāb Wa'īd Man Iqtaṭ'a Ḥaqq al-Muslim bi Yamīn Fājiratin bi al-Nār.

[186] See, Muslim, *Ṣaḥīḥ*, Kitāb al-Īmān, Bāb Wa'īd Man Iqtaṭ'a Ḥaqq al-Muslim bi Yamīn Fājiratin bi al-Nār.

[187] See, Muslim, *Ṣaḥīḥ*, Kitāb al-Birr wa 'l-Ṣilah wa 'l-Ādāb, Bāb Ṣilat al-Raḥim.

This claim is uglier than the opinion of the Khārijīs who accused those who committed sins with disbelief, the Mu'tazilah and others. The invalidity of this opinion is known by necessity in the religion of Islam, and the proofs for this are confirmed in places other than here.

The second: to abandon forming opinions and actions based upon what is required by the *ḥadīth*s of the Messenger of Allah (peace be on him), assuming that to argue according to them leads to the defamation of those who contravened those *ḥadīth*s. Yet this abandonment would lead to misguidance and following in the footsteps of the People of the Book who have taken their rabbis and their monks and the Messiah, the son of Mary (peace be on him and her), as lords besides Allah, as the Prophet (peace be on him) said, "They did not worship them, [meaning their monks and rabbis], but these monks and rabbis made lawful to them what Allah has forbidden, and prohibited what Allah has made lawful, and they obeyed them in this."[188] Thus, this abandonment leads to obeying the created ones in disobedience to the Creator. It also leads to an ugly result and incorrect interpretations. This could be understood from the implied meaning of the statement of the Exalted, ❨*Obey Allah, and obey the Messenger, and those charged with authority among you. If you differ in anything among yourselves, refer it to Allah and His Messenger, if you do believe in Allah and the Last Day. That is better and fairer in the end*❩.[189]

The scholars differ in various issues. If every tradition containing sternness (*taghlīz*), which was opposed by someone meant that this *taghlīz* would be abandoned or that the tradition would not be acted upon, then the outcome necessitated by this (which is the abandonment of the *ḥadīth*s of the Prophet) would be greater in enormity than to attribute someone with disbelief or abandonment of the religion. If this feared outcome (i.e. abandonment of the *ḥadīth*s of the Prophet) was not greater than what was before it (i.e. attributing someone with disbelief or abandonment of the religion), it will certainly not be inferior to it.

Therefore, it is a must for us to believe in the entire Book (the Qur'ān) and to follow all that was revealed by Allah to us. And we should not believe in a part of the Book and disbelieve in another part. Our hearts should not be inclined to follow some of the *Sunnah* and avoid following some of it on the basis of customs and desires. This would indeed be an abandonment of the straight path in preference to the way of those who have brought wrath upon themselves, and those who have gone astray.   May Allah guide us to what He loves and is pleasing to Him in terms of speech and action in a state of

---

[188] See, al-Ṭabarī, *Tafsīr*, 10: 114; 'Abd al-Raḥmān Ibn Abī Ḥātim, *Tafsīr al-Qur'ān* (Ṣaydā: al-Maktabat al-'Aṣriyyah, n.d.), 6: 1784; al-Bayhaqī, *Sunan*, 10: 116.
[189] Qur'ān 4: 59.

goodness and well-being for us and all Muslims. And praise be to Allah the Lord of the worlds, and countless salutations and blessings be upon Muhammad, the seal of the Prophets, and upon his family and his righteous Companions and his wives, the Mothers of the Believers, and those who follow them in goodness till the Day of Judgement.[190]

---

[190] The translation of this text was based on the edition of *Raf' al-Malām 'an al-'Aimmat al-A'lām* (Riyadh: al-Ri'āsah al-'Āmmah li Idārāt al-Buḥūth al-'Ilmiyyah, 1413 AH). The opinions expressed in the translated text are those of the author, Ibn Taymiyyah, and not necessarily those of the translator.

www.ingramcontent.com/pod-product-compliance
Lightning Source LLC
Chambersburg PA
CBHW061301140726
47998CB00006B/2322